The
101st AIRBORNE
From Holland to
Hitler's Eagle's Nest

D1628584

Mark Bando

Motorbooks International
Publishers & Wholesalers ®

Dedication

*This book is dedicated to the Mothers, Wives, Sweethearts and Sisters
of the men who didn't come back.
With the dedication, a prayer that some answers will be found herein.*

In Memoriam

*To Joseph Lawrence Logan, a great personality and talent, who was KIA with the 25th Inf. Div. in Vietnam, spring, 1969.
He didn't live long enough to write his war book. May Joe symbolize the tragic loss of thousands of great Americans who
have perished in wars through the ages. They are gone, but not forgotten.*

First published in 1995 by Motorbooks International
Publishers & Wholesalers, PO Box 2, 729 Prospect
Avenue, Osceola, WI 54020 USA

Library of Congress Cataloging-in-Publication Data
Bando, Mark.
    The 101st. Airborne: from Holland to Hitler's eagle
nest/Mark Bando.
    p. cm.
    Includes index.
    ISBN 0-7603-0156-5 (pbk.)
    1. World War, 1939–1945—Campaigns—Western
Front. 2. United States. Army. Airborne Division,
101st—History. I. Title.
D756.3.B36   1995
940.54′4973—dc20   95-36438
ISBN 0-7603-0156-5

On the front cover: Officers of I/502 in Holland in
September 1944. Pictured from left to right are Lt. Corey
Shepard, Capt. Champ L. Baker, Ed Augustinowski, Bob
Burns, and Lt. Robert B. Molsberry. *Molsberry*

On the back cover: (top) These HQ/501 survivors
proudly display a bullet-riddled sign. Standing, left to
right: Waldo Brown, Jim Ganter, Belgian civilian, R. J.
Wilbur, Dave Smith, Chief Sayers, Joe Sloan
(photographer), and Budd. Front, left to right: Eugene
Amburgey, W. C. Dunn, Ted Becker, Bill Canfield
(holding sign), and Duane Henson. *Sloan*

On the back cover: (bottom) Two members of 3rd
Platoon, F/501 man a 1919A4 LMG on the dike near the
windmill west of Heteren in October 1944. A small road
ran perpendicular to the dike here. At left is Emerson
Rhodes, who recalls that his large mesh helmet net was
then out of style in the 501. At right is Taylor Sharp.
Krochka

Printed and bound in the United States of America

Contents

Acknowledgments

This is a companion volume to my first book: *The 101st Airborne At Normandy*. One of the greatest joys in collecting World War II memorabilia is that of sharing discoveries with other enthusiasts. Photographs and "war stories" lend themselves splendidly to that purpose.

The generously shared recollections of hundreds of surviving World War II Screaming Eagles has certainly been the *sine qua non* of these compendiums of fact and folklore. The research has spanned a quarter of a century, and those interviewed are too numerous to mention individually.

However, in this work, the prodigious efforts of divisional photographers Albert A. Krochka and Mike Musura must again be credited. Caroline Krochka has been great in giving unlimited access to her late husband's photo collection.

Joe "Gopher" Sloan, who replaced Krochka late in the war as 501st photographer, could not be located, but evidence of his work will also be found in this book.

I am indebted to two Dutch historians, Geurt and Coby DeHaartog, of Zetten, Holland, for graciously touring me around sites I never would have found without them in 1989.

Adequate tribute could never be paid to my patient and gentle wife, Candace Ann and her family for their assistance and encouragement.

Before listing the outstanding contributors to this book, I would like to state that it has been a great personal honor for me to meet and associate with men who made such a lasting and immortal contribution to American history.

Contributors to this book include:

Frank Anness (506), Fred Bahlau (506), Fred Baynes (501), Jerry Beam (506), Carl Beck (501), Ed Benecke (377), Bruce Beyer (501), Tony Borelli (506), Charles Carlsen (501), Steve Chappuis (502), John Cipolla (501), Herb Clark (506), Earl Cox (502), Joe Crilley (326), Grayson Davis (401), Carl Dickinson (327), Paul Dovholuk (502), Jim Duggins (501), Charles E.S. Eckman (501), Johnny Gibson (506), Leo Gillis (501), Bob Granche (326), Ian Hamilton (501), Fred Hancock (502), Sammie Homan (501), John Hopke (501), Ray Hood (502), Ed Hughes (501), Allen Hurd (501), Glenn Johnson (502), Bill Kennedy (506), George Koskimaki (SIGNAL), Dick Ladd (502), Anacleto Leone (501), Gus Liapes (506), Robert Lott (401), Patrick Macri (SIGNAL), James Marshall (501), Jim Martin (506), Robert Martin (506), Melton McMorries (501), Bill Meeker (327), Werner Meier (501), Steve Mihok (506), Frank Miller (502), Harry Mole (501), Robert Molsberry (502), Herm Moulliet (506), Chuck O'Neill (501), Frank Palys (506), Joe Pangerl (502), Art Parker (377), Ken Parker (506), Ed Pieczatowski (327), Leo Premetz (327), John Primerano (501), Bob Reeves (506), Chuck Ritzler (501), Dick Rowles (501), Bill Russo (501), Ed Sapinski (502), Bill Sefton (501), Cecil L. Simmons (502), Adam Slusher (326), Mort Smit (502), Bernard Sterno (502), Don Straith (506), Len Swartz (502), Paul Teator (HO), John Tocco (326), David White (502), R.J. Wilbur (501), and Dick Winters (506).

Foreword

Those acquainted with the numerous history-making events in which the 101st Airborne was involved in the last ten months of WWII will appreciate the massive amount that has been written on the subject. Why another book?

This book combines numerous personal accounts, many previously untold, with over 200 rare photos that help illustrate the locales and persons mentioned in the narrative. While some of the "big picture" is described herein, the basic format of this book is to tell in detail what a few individuals experienced in each battle, to convey the personal "flavor" of the fight and the men who made history at Market-Garden and Bastogne. Captured German documents and correspondence shed new light on the enemy side of the story.

This is a "human history," thanks to the generously shared experiences of over 700 WWII veterans of the 101st. For those wishing greater detail and more of the big picture, the books by S.L.A. Marshall, George Koskimaki, Rapport-Northwood, Critchell, Ambrose, Webster, and a host of others should be consulted. Don Burgett's book on Bastogne from a single rifleman's perspective will hopefully be in print soon, also.

In a book of this size, only limited space can be devoted to each phase of the five campaigns included in its scope. No attempt has been made, nor claim attached, that these contents are anywhere near a comprehensive accounting of those campaigns.

The stories and photos herein represent the highlights of many years of research, and I trust the reader will find the narrative as readable and fascinating as are the men who lived them.

—Mark A. Bando
Detroit, Michigan, 1994

Chapter One

English Summer

Members of the 101st Airborne Div. who had survived the Normandy invasion without serious wounds, were returned to the England in July 1944. The official casualty list indicates 868 men were KIA, hundreds more were missing in German POW camps, and the number of wounded was in the thousands. The picture was grim, but gradually, many of the wounded trickled back from

"I Promise You Another Mission"
On 31 August 1944 another mission took the troopers of the 101st as far as the airfields before the mission was canceled. General Maxwell D. Taylor (above) assembled the division, apologized, and promised the troops another mission. Someone booed. Lieutenant G. W. Sefton of HQ/2 501 later commented: "I could never understand how anyone as obviously brilliant as Maxwell Taylor could overlook the enlisted man's point of view so far as to assume that every private, non-com, and junior officer there was just as anxious to return to combat as he, a West Point general, was." *Musura*

hospitals, and even a few of the MIAs miraculously rejoined the unit.

Sergeant Ed Hughes of F/501 had been wounded near Angoville and evacuated to England before the bulk of the division returned. When he met a bus containing the survivors of his 2nd Platoon, only 12 men got off.

"Where are the rest?," he asked Chuck O'Neill.

"This is it; there are no more."

Johnny Gibson of HQ/3 506 had been captured just above Carentan on D-day in a group with George Rosie and others. Gibson was a medic and unwounded, and the Germans used him to treat their own casualties as they retreated south. The Germans were so lacking in medical supplies that they were boiling and re-using gauze pads. Mercurochrome and crepe paper was the only dressing available to cover wounds. Gibson eventually was transferred to Stalag 221 at Rennes. This was a bit of good fortune, as Rennes was liberated on 4 August 1944, releasing Gibson and others, most of whom were badly wounded and ZI'd (sent to the Zone of Interior, or the USA). Gibson was ready for more action and returned to his battalion, in which he would serve until badly wounded in the Bulge.

The 101st had had its baptism of fire in Normandy, and most importantly from a psychological standpoint, had taken the measure of the German soldier and his capabilities.

Lieutenant William J. Russo of 2/501 later remarked:

No Thanks, General
What General Taylor saw. Note the ambivalent facial expressions of the troops.

I think they (the Germans) had gotten so used to their terror—you know, scare the shit out of everybody in Poland, the low countries, Russia. They got onto terrorizing this and terrorizing that . . . well when you meet people who don't terrorize, you're up shit creek. It all goes the other way, really.

They used to drop us those [propaganda] pamphlets in Holland and Bastogne: "If you don't give up right now, you know, that this is gonna happen and that is gonna happen . . ." Best toilet paper we ever had! [Laughs] Ahhh, that was comical.

A Holy War

Certainly, casualties were always considered, and the troopers worried more for their families than themselves. Transfers out were available, but to most troopers, the only honorable way out was through death or the "million-dollar wound," which would send them home. As a handful of survivors made it through each future battle, they came to view themselves as "fugitives from the law of averages." Yet, they continued to face whatever was in store for them. Carl Beck of H/501 said, "This war was viewed as a crusade against evil. Therefore, do your part in the crusade."

Lee Parrish of G/501 had survived the nightmare of Normandy, including a knife fight with a German paratrooper he had encountered while getting water from a stream.

"I wasn't much of a soldier until I accepted the fact that I was just a dead man, walking around, waiting to find out where I was going to lie down for good," he said after the war. "Once I accepted that fact, I became a fairly decent combat soldier."

Another Canceled Jump
Corporal Harold Bice and Pfc. Lyman Allen Hurd, preparing to board their plane in England on 17 August 1944. The troops were assembled and sealed off at airfields and issued ammunition, rations, and French currency, but the jump was canceled. The 101st was to land in position to help close the Falaise Pocket, but General Patton's armored forces arrived so quickly that the mission was rendered unnecessary. Although the men have been issued the new quick-release T-7 parachute harnesses and combat boots, they still wear the gas impregnated M42 jump suits. These men belonged to 2/501's S-2 Section. *Beyer*

The fear of being maimed and surviving may have been greater than the fear of death. Don Burgett of A/506 gave an insight into the philosophy that helped him to function. Asked how he overcame his fear of being shot in the head when raising up from cover to return fire in a shoot-out, Don remarked: "Well, look at it this way—if you *did* get hit in the head, you wouldn't have anything to worry about."

Chapter Two

Market-Garden Plan and Marshalling Areas

During the summer of 1944, the First Allied Airborne Army was born, under command of Gen. Lewis H. Brereton (US Army Air Forces). This Army included the British 1st and 6th Airborne divisions, the US 82nd and 101st Airborne Div., and would later include also the 17th Airborne Div. The latter US divisions constituted the US 18th Airborne Corps, under Gen. Matthew Ridgeway.

Order of Battle, 101st Airborne Division, 1944

Although listed as a full division on paper, the 101st Airborne was down to about 12,000 men after many of those wounded in the Normandy invasion had recovered and returned to their units and replacements had been incorporated. The division consisted of 101st HQ Company (HQ/101), Signal Company, Recon Platoon, and Military Police (MP) Platoon; the 501st, 502nd, and 506th Parachute Inf. Reg. (generally referred to as the 501, the 502, and the 506); the 327th Glider Inf. Reg. (the 327); the 1st Bn. of the 401st Glider Inf. Bn. (the 1/401); the 326th Airborne Eng. Bn. (the 326); the 377th Parachute Field Artillery Bn. (the 377); the 321st Glider Artillery Bn. (the 321); the 907th Glider Field Artillery Bn. (the 907); the 81st Airborne Artillery Antitank Bn. (the 81); the 326th Airborne Medical Company; and the 426th Airborne Quartermaster Company.

The Market-Garden Plan

Field Marshall Montgomery wielded considerable political clout in the coalition of Western allies and insisted finally that his grandiose scheme to end the war before Christmas be implemented. The plan, called Market-Garden (Market was the airborne assault and Garden the ground offensive) would use the First Allied Airborne Army to jump at intervals along a highway extending through the current front line, deep into Holland. A number of bridges were to be seized and held by the airborne troops as Monty's Guards Armored Div. raced northward to Arnhem. In mitigation, Monty wanted to drop his British 1st Airborne troops in the northernmost spot, at Arnhem, but the end result would be "a 50mi salient leading nowhere," as one critic called it. Indeed the entire plan was perhaps doomed to fail in reaching its ultimate goal, and this could have been predicted based on Monty's record thus far since D-day. His ground forces had never moved rapidly forward in anything like the lightning thrusts needed to make Market-Garden a success.

In theory, if Monty's armor had reached the bridge at Arnhem in time, it would have pivoted eastward and drove straight toward Berlin to overthrow the Hitler regime at its nerve center. This maneuver also would've bypassed the Roer Valley and the Siegfried Line defenses of Hitler's West Wall, but to discuss what was hoped for is now idle speculation.

The US Airborne survivors of this operation are of course cynical about the sacrifices of their buddies and the heavy losses sustained with questionable gain, but each engagement was a toe-to-toe confrontation with the enemy. Each encounter was thus fought accordingly. Any local victory, no matter how small was viewed as bringing the war in Europe one bit close to an end. Some of the American

Captain Cecil Simmons
Simmons, with his stick from HQ/502 on 17 September. The 4U marking on the nose of the C-47 identifies it as a part of the 89th TCS, 438th TCG. Also visible in the photo is Sgt. Fred Patheiger. Flak damage (possibly from the recent Southern France invasion) is evident on the side, below the cockpit. *Pangerl*

troopers who survived this mission complain that the ultimate failure of the mission was due to factors having nothing to do with them. As they truthfully point out, all their assigned missions were accomplished and in short order. Yet few will actively fault the dedication or courage of their British and Commonwealth comrades in the battle. The sacrifices and skill of these warriors was evident at every hand.

The British Army had its strengths (especially the artillery, which was accurate and timely) and its weaknesses (mainly tactical and procedural), and these factors would become very evident to the members of the 101st Airborne in the coming fight in the Netherlands.

Thus, with little time for plans or preparation, the 101st was to drop between Son (sometimes spelled "Zon") and St. Oedenrode, and also in the Veghel area, to open a corridor for Monty's armor.

Issue Of New Equipment
By the time the 101st troops actually entered the Netherlands in Operation Market-Garden, their overall look had changed notably from their look in Normandy. New-version jumpsuits issued in late 1944 were actually the standard M43 combat suit, green in color instead of tan, with rectangular pockets and a sateen finish. Actually, the Army was undergoing an elimination of all nonstandard uniforms and footwear. Jumpsuits were no longer to be worn and were actually recalled in some units. Many troopers hid a set in the bottom of their barracks bags, to be used later. Jump boots were also nonstandard and were to be replaced with the recently introduced two-buckle combat boots.

The only thing making the paratrooper look different from a regular infantryman at that point was the addition of cargo pockets to the upper legs of the M43 combat trousers, thus converting them to jump trousers of a sort. The parachute riggers were put to work making these conversions of canvas material, and tie-down straps were also sewn on to help secure the load. Many troopers considered the straps a nuisance and cut them off.

A new cap patch for the overseas cap was also introduced, incorporating the parachute and glid-

Combat Jumpsuits—Old and New
In 1944, Giles Thurman (left) modeled the M42 tan jump-suit (this example is reinforced). His buddy wears the new green M43 combat suit, modified by riggers with cargo pockets and tie-downs on the legs. *H. Moulliet*

Creased Skull
Sergeant Ed Pieczatowski of G/327 in England, summer of 1944, displays the helmet shot off his head by an SS trooper near Montmartin-en-Graignes in Normandy. The slug creased Ed's skull and knocked him down, but he was not seriously wounded. This happened to Ed a second time at Bastogne, with the same result. Such close calls became commonplace among the Screaming Eagles. *Pieczatowski*

er—red for artillery and blue for infantry—all in one patch. Paratroopers immediately balked loudly at wearing a patch with a glider superimposed over their parachute and in some units (notably the 502), refused to wear the new patch until close to VE-day. There was a distinct feeling that all this standardization was unnecessary and a suspicion that it was brought on more by jealousy than any other factor. The jump boots, M42 suits, and cap patch had been definite status symbols, unique to the parachute troops, and now the Army was taking them away.

Of all these take-aways, only the jump boots were eventually restored. There was, after all, a safety factor involved in the wearing of jump boots. They had been designed to offer support to the ankles on landing from a jump, and the buckles that protruded from the combat boots could easily snag on a suspension line in event of poor body position

upon leaving the plane. All manner of malfunctions could be imagined.

Unlike the issue of the smaller, gauze arm flags, which had been only spotily issued for the Normandy jump, all troops of the 101st entering Holland were issued with an armband printed on oilcloth. This larger brassard was issued with two steel safety pins, and although it was made with numerous holes punched in it to facilitate securing to the upper arm with string, it was usually folded and pinned on the sleeve.

New helmet nets, reputed to be of British manufacture, were also issued having a mesh between 1/4 and 1/2in. These were noticeably different from the wide-mesh (1in) nets worn in Normandy. It became fashionable to wear the new net with a paratrooper's cloth first-aid kit tied to the front, although HQ/501 would soon publish a memo banning the

"The Greatest All-Around Machine-Gunner the War has Produced"

Private Melton "Tex" McMorries joined G/501 as a replacement before Market-Garden and was soon to establish himself as one of the deadliest gunners in the 101st Airborne.

Like all good gunners, Tex would adjust the mills and traversing mechanism on his weapon when setting up at an anticipated killing ground. When the attackers came-in, he usually found them to approach on an oblique angle, rather than directly toward him. He would use the swivel tripod to advantage and start firing in front of each enemy target, swinging the gun in toward the man, instead of merely leading him. Thus, the bullet dispersion would usually find its target. "This could make the difference between a hit or a miss," he said.

Tex also felt that instinct and common sense had a lot to do with a machine-gunner's success in battle, and he said, "A smart sharpshooter would score more kills than a dumb expert."

By the time the 101st was pulled out of Holland, Tex McMorries had scored such an impressive string of victories that Lt. Col. Julian Ewell selected him to be the main instructor for new machine-gunners joining the 501.

In introducing McMorries to a class of replacement gunners, Lt. Jack Cranford said:

> You are all well trained in machine-gunnery; many of you are experienced. We can help you only a little more, but this little can save your life or turn the tide of battle. You need courage and skill. We can only help you with the latter. Mac is the greatest all-around machine-gunner the war has produced. He has many times turned almost certain defeat into victory. With the use of his skill and courage, he has killed more enemy than many of you will ever see, so try to learn a little more.

Tex McMorries was tall, lanky, and part Apache. Some of the events described in the Holland and Bastogne battles will help demonstrate how he gained his reputation.

Tex McMorries, Super Machine-Gunner
Melton "Tex" McMorries, the G/501 machine-gunner who was twice recommended for the DSC but never received the medal. *Doris McMorries*

practice. Photographic evidence indicates that it continued to flourish in the 502, even into the Bulge era.

Probably the most important change in equipment for the average jumper was the adoption by the US Army of the quick-release parachute harness. This consisted of a round metal disc that could be rotated and slapped to instantly release three of the four harness straps of the main parachute.

Initially, this arrangement (designated as the T-7 harness) was sewn by riggers onto the existing T-5 harnesses to replace the clip fasteners used in Normandy and on earlier jumps.

Ironically, the quick-release mechanism was invented and patented by the American Switlik Parachute Co., but was used first by British paratroops in Normandy. After numerous complaints were lodged about the tightening-up of the T-5 harness and the slowness in removing it in combat, the US Army finally embraced the quick-release design.

Photographic evidence indicates this arrangement was worn to the airfields for the jumps that were canceled in the summer of 1944, prior to Holland. Worn in combination with them were the M42 jumpsuit and the combat boots.

Another American jumping device that made its combat debut in Market-Garden, was the leg bag for heavy equipment, which was jumped attached to one leg and released before landing to dangle below the descending jumper on a 15–20ft rope. This enabled the heavy equipment (which could be a radio,

Malfunction Junction
Injured on a practice jump in England are John Cipolla (C/501), Lt. Ed Defelice (B/501), and Lt. Joe Wasco (G/

501). As a lieutenant colonel commanding 2nd Bn., 327th Inf. in the Vietnam War, Wasco distinguished himself in battle.

machine gun [MG], or bazooka) to land before the jumper did.

On the Normandy drop, American paratroopers used a British-made bag for this purpose, which was lowered by rope after one's chute opened. But during the summer, M/Sgt. Joe Lanci of the 501st's Parachute Maintenance section invented a more sophisticated gadget that the Americans would later mass-produce and call their own. This bag incorporated a ripcord that enabled a jumper to drop the bag by pulling the handle after his main chute had deployed.

Colonel Howard Johnson, the 501st CO, recognized the significance of this enduring contribution to the airborne, and wrote Lanci up for the Legion of Merit medal, which he did receive.

Although the 1919A-6 light machine gun (LMG) was introduced at this time with carrying handle and bipod added, many gunners preferred the wider, faster traverse afforded by the tripod-mounted 1919A-4.

Chapter Three

The Flight Across and the Jump— Drop Zones Son, Eerde, and Heeswijk

Due to the short notice before Market-Garden was launched, the troops participating received much shorter briefings than they had before Normandy. But the survivors of D-day now knew what to expect of combat. Experience had taught them to leave much unnecessary equipment behind, so many troopers were dropping with a lighter load than they had borne in Normandy.

Charlie Eckman, the intrepid warrior of HQ/2 501's LMG Platoon recalled: "My buddies and I gathered together, nicked our fingers with knives, and mingled our blood. We swore we would fight to the death for each other."

After crossing the Channel, planes bearing 101st Airborne paratroopers would turn left and head north along the European continent, crossing the front lines near the Belgian-Dutch border, then dropping their cargo along the road that would become known as "Hell's Highway."

The 82nd Airborne, flying a different (northern) route, would land just below the British near Grave and Nijmegen. Drop zones (DZ) A and A-1 for the 101st were below the 82nd's area, near Veghel and Eerde, Holland. These troops would land shortly after 1300hr, followed by the 506th troops dropping on DZ C, just above Son, Holland. The 502 would come in last just above the 506 at the north edge of the same field, south of St. Oedenrode. The 326th Medical Company with 52 personnel and a surgical team, would land on landing zone (LZ) W in the center of the same field, along with elements of the 327 and miscellaneous HQ units. Airborne engineers and gliderborne artillery would also land on LZ W. Of the 377th artillery, only B Battery jumped, landing on DZ C two days later.

On 17 September, troop-carrier planes departing England from Aldermaston, Chilbolton, Membury, Welford, and Chilton-Foliat, would deliver 6,641 troopers in 424 C-47s.

When Lt. Bill Sefton's plane, bearing a stick of D/501, got airborne, he saw the men nod at each other. As if by signal, they all reached down and unfastened the two buckles on each of their combat boots, The flaps fell off and dropped to the floor. This revealed them all to be wearing jump boots, contrary to pre-flight orders. To comply, they had cut the flaps off their combat boots, buckled them around their ankles, then disposed of the objectionable flaps as soon as they got airborne.

General Taylor had personally requested that Maj. Hank Hannah, formerly S-3 of 506, be moved up to division G-3. He was on a plane to Holland in that capacity when the C-47 was hit by flak. Hannah wrote in his journal:

> When we passed over the British Second Army and into hostile territory, the flak commenced raining on us from Eindhoven. My plane was hit in the left engine and left tail section, and some of it came through the floor at the front of the plane where no one was seated. The fire became so intense that the motor cut out, and we had to jump prematurely. However, the pilot held on so tenaciously that we were able to jump within the edge of the DZ. The crew chief jumped out after we had gone (I saw him in Son later), but the plane went down in flames. I

Airborne General
On 17 September, Gen. Maxwell D. Taylor (second from left), CO of the 101st Airborne Div., adjusts his reserve chute as Lt. Col. Pat Cassidy (second from right), CO of 1/502 looks on. Note the cuffs of Taylor's M43 jacket, evidently a prototype or experimental model. *US Army*

VIP Transport
Pasaaic Warrior is the nose art of this B-17 Flying Fortress, which was the personal plane of Gen. Lewis Brereton of the First Allied Airborne Army. General Brereton flew in this fortress along with the C-47s laden with paratroopers. He was able to witness the drop from his personal plane on 17 September 1944. A few days later, Brereton was on the ground and moving up Hell's Highway to confer personally with his various commanders on the ground. *Simmons*

Second D-Day
General Brereton waves to his troopers as they prepare for their second D-day. *Musura*

haven't learned about the pilot, co-pilot and navigator, but I'm afraid they didn't make it—perhaps because they stuck it out for us.

Mishaps at DZ A

Due to the shot-down pathfinder plane that was to mark DZ A-1 between the canal and the Aa river west of Veghel, Lt. Ian Hamilton's battalion was misdropped some distance farther west. The Drop at DZ A-1 was at 400ft. Despite the wrong location, 1/501 landed in a compact area, assembled quickly, and moved on to Veghel with few casualties. Father Francis Sampson, Catholic chaplain of the 501, landed in the moat of Heeswijk Castle. Captain William Burd of HQ/501 was left behind with a rear guard to cover 1/501's withdrawal. Burd was killed, and most of the rear guard was wiped-out.

Members of 2/ and 3/501 had the ideal jump onto sandy plowed fields near Eerde. Ground fire was minimal, and the troopers bailed out between 1,000 and 1,200ft in altitude. Inevitably, as in any mass combat jump, a few individuals experienced problems.

Lieutenant Bill Sefton of HQ/2 501's S-2 (intelligence) section had decided to make the jump with a fully assembled M-1 Garand rifle cradled in his arms. Approaching the DZ, Sefton was "not altogether sure I could keep my breakfast down." At the green light, Sefton exited his plane at a long thrust, holding the M-1. As his suspension lines were de-

ploying, one wrapped around the muzzle of his rifle, just behind the front sight. After the chute opened, Sefton looked up to see his rifle dangling from just below the skirt of his canopy. Upon landing, Sefton ducked his head and heard the rifle hit

Doomed Trooper
Swamped with equipment and parachutes on 17 September is Joe Mero, a former layout man for a Long Island newspaper. Mero, a clerk in HQ/2 501, was married and would lose his life after heroic fighting in the Veghel area. *Baynes*

Ritzler and Maguire
Ready to load up on 17 September are Chuck Ritzler (left) and Walt Maguire (right), both of D/501. Note the exten-sion added to Maguire's Griswold Bag, enabling him to jump with his M-1 rifle fully assembled. *Ritzler*

Marshaling at Membury
Gus Liapes snapped this photo of two of his buddies before takeoff. John Grispan (left) lost a limb in Holland but survived WWII; he has since passed away. Charles Dickey (right) from St. Louis, Missouri, was, according to Liapes, "the bravest man I have ever known. His twin brother was killed on the Dieppe raid. He was always at my side or after a Kraut." Dickey was KIA in Holland. Both Dickey and Liapes had been wounded twice in Normandy. *Liapes*

the ground nearby.

Most of the injuries sustained by jumpers on DZ A were caused by jumpers being struck by their own weapons, worn disassembled in a Griswold Bag, tucked at an angle across their chest, or beneath the reserve parachute. In many cases, the weapon bag would straighten into a vertical position from the opening shock. The trooper, too distracted by his surroundings to notice, would hit the ground, at which time his knees drove the bag rapidly upward into his face.

A trooper from F/501 named Joe Lamber was making his first combat jump that day. Joe's main chute seriously malfunctioned, failing to open. Joe pulled his reserve chest pack ripcord, but his deploying reserve chute wrapped around his main streamer. Joe was falling to a certain death when an equipment bundle below him, filled with weapons, oscillated into his path. Joe struck this shock-absorbing device so hard he was knocked unconscious. But he floated safely to the ground, draped across the bundle. A surgeon who had watched the incident unfold, revived Joe on the ground and explained to him how he had arrived intact.

Hayden Faulk was another member of F/501.

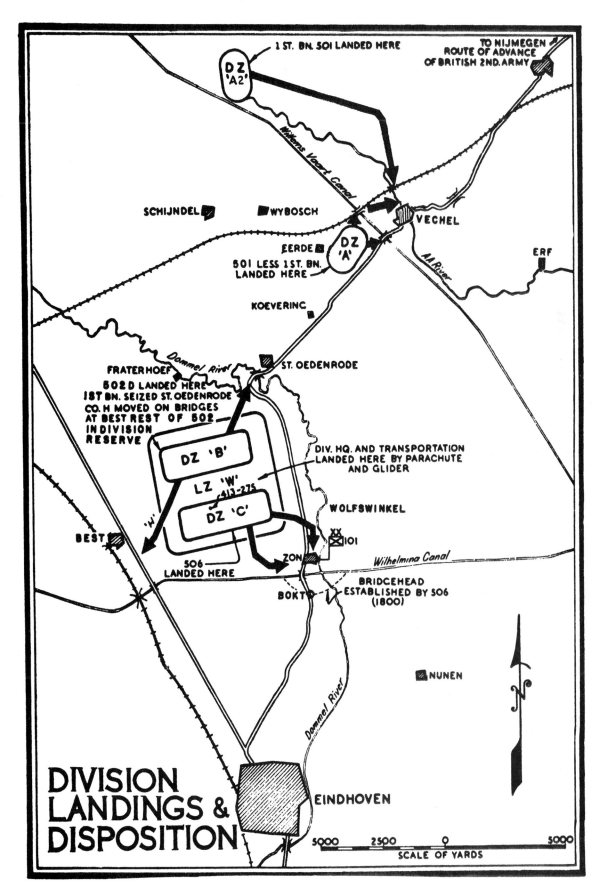

1 ST. BN. 501 LANDED HERE

TO NIJMEGEN
ROUTE OF ADVANCE
OF BRITISH 2ND. ARMY

DZ 'A2'

SCHIJNDEL

WYBOSCH

VECHEL

EERDE

DZ 'A'

ERF

501 LESS 1ST. BN.
LANDED HERE

A A River

KOEVERINC

FRATERHOEF

Dommel River

ST. OEDENRODE

502 D LANDED HERE
1ST BN. SEIZED ST. OEDENRODE
CO. H MOVED ON BRIDGES
AT BEST REST OF 502
IN DIVISION
RESERVE

DIV. HQ. AND TRANSPORTATION
LANDED HERE BY PARACHUTE
AND GLIDER

DZ 'B'

LZ 'W'
413-275

WOLFSWINKEL

'W'

DZ 'C'

XX 101

BEST

ZON

Wilhelmina Canal

506
LANDED HERE

BRIDGEHEAD
ESTABLISHED BY 506
(1800)

BOKTD

NUNEN

N

Dommel River

DIVISION
LANDINGS &
DISPOSITION

EINDHOVEN

5000   2500   0   5000
SCALE OF YARDS

HQ/502
Members of HQ/502 at their marshaling area in England.

Several members of the S-2 section are visible in the foreground. *Musura*

Faulk jumped with one of Sergeant Lanci's new leg bags containing an LMG. After the opening shock, Faulk was twisted around in his harness, such that he couldn't reach the ripcord to release the bundle from his leg. To make matters worse, Faulk was

Trooper Taxi
A plane of the 89th TCS, 438th TCG, ready for takeoff. *Krochka*

drifting toward the only Dutch house for hundreds of yards around. Faulk crashed right through the roof of the house with the gun attached to his leg, breaking the instep of his foot. He eventually limped into Veghel and collapsed in the town.

Harold Paulson recalled a mishap that occurred on DZ A-1. One of Paulson's C/501 buddies, named Francis Beavers landed in a tall tree, from which he dangled upside down, unable to free himself. Due to the height of the tree, his buddies were unable to get him down. Beavers was left behind and was taken prisoner by the Germans.

DZ C—Son, Holland

The wide-open expanse above Son provided an ample space for two DZs B and C, plus glider LZ W. Soon after the 506 came to ground, glider serials began to land, with medical, HQ, and artillery elements.

Don Burgett of A/506 landed on DZ C and provided a narrative describing some details of the flight and the jump:

We took off and circled as the planes gathered in formation. We were at a higher altitude than on the Normandy jump. I recall looking out the left side of the plane and seeing the white cliffs of Dover; they looked about an inch high. We were really up in altitude.

"This Yellow Bastard Won't Get the Honor of Jumping Into Battle with You Brave Men!"

Lieutenant Ian Hamilton of B/501 was a Normandy veteran who recalled that he penciled-in a last-minute replacement on the jump manifest for his plane. This soldier was a boxer and apparently a tough guy. As the C-47 was taxiing along the runway for takeoff, the replacement intentionally fired the carbine in his leg scabbard. The bullet went clear through one of his feet and out the open door of the plane.

The aircraft was picking up speed for takeoff, but Hamilton grabbed the trooper by his harness and dragged him close to the open door of the plane.

Hamilton faced his stick and bellowed: "This yellow bastard won't get the honor of jumping into battle with you brave men!"

With that, Hamilton flung the trooper out of the moving plane and he thumped and bounced along the runway, to be retrieved by medics on the ground.

Following the campaign, a Board of Inquiry was convened at Mourmelon to investigate the incident. After testimony was heard, Hamilton was ruled justified in his action that day.

17 Sept, 1944, a "stick" of paratroopers enroute to Holland. *Krochka*

Going across Europe, we really received no antiaircraft fire. It was a beautiful sunny fall day.

We got the red light signaling that we were approaching the DZ. Everybody stood up and hooked-up. We took up a jump attitude near the DZ, and we began to receive flak. Not as much MG fire as in Normandy, but a lot of 88's. I saw a couple of planes go down.

The tall young blond trooper in front of me was of Polish descent and had recently transferred to the paratroops from the ski troops. He looked out to the port and said: "Is that flak?" I said, "Yeah. Look out there; you can see it exploding." About that time, a hole appeared in our port wing, maybe 2-1/2ft wide and about 4–6ft long. It's strange. You see the surface of the wing. It's there, and all of a sudden it disappears; you don't even see the metal leaving. So there was this big hole there, and this ski trooper said, "Let's get out of this damned thing!" We got the signal to go, and we went.

I learned later from Sergeant Vetland that the trooper behind me didn't jump. He froze in the door and Vetland hit him real hard and knocked him to one side and the trooper went back to England on the plane. The man tried—he had battle fatigue and should have been treated accordingly, but of course he wasn't.

After the opening shock, we had plenty of time. This was the first time we jumped with the quick release. All the planes kept tight formation and maintained proper altitude despite heavy flak. The troop-carrier crews were right on the ball on this one. A plane near me was hit and losing altitude. I got down on the field and met Phillips and a few of the others.

On the Normandy drop some guys had been killed on the ground before they could get out of their chute, so on this drop the guys had the quick release. A lot of 'em wanted to get out of it in a hurry, so they had the safety clip undone, and some even had the release disc twisted. A tap on it after that and three of the straps would drop away. They also had their belly band off; that way when they hit the ground, all they had to do was unclip the reserve chute, hit this thing, and it would fall off.

Well one of the guys . . . his chute opened and he came out of the chute; the chute drifted off by itself. The guy came down without a chute at all, hit the thatched roof of a haystack, ricocheted, and hit the ground. You could see his arms and legs windmilling, and they kept getting smaller. All his bones were breaking.

I was with Doc Saint, our medic from New York. I asked him, "Are you going to him?"He looked and said, "Aint no sense in going to *that* one."

Descending on Son
A view from above, shows one serial of the 101st dropping above Son, Holland, 17 September 1944. *Hood*

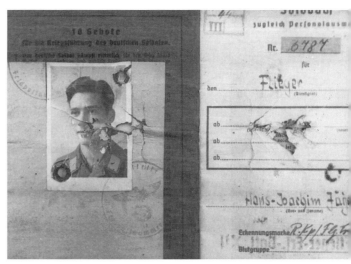

First Blood
The owner of this pay book, a German soldier of Flak Reg. 53, had the dubious honor of being the first enemy soldier killed by B/506 in Holland. Note bullet holes through inside of front cover. *Clark*

About 35ft above our head, two gliders were trying to get into the same field. One was above the other. The lower one's right wing hit the left trailing edge of the one up above. He spun, made a quarter turn, and hit the road. The jeep broke loose and came forward. The other glider spun out the other way, and he went down.

We stopped to try and get the survivors out. I was on my knees trying to break some plexiglass when someone said "We got a mission. We gotta be there," so we left as others were working on the wreckage. [Burgett's mission was to seize the bridge at Son over the Wilhelmina Canal.]

Winner Take All

The A/506 set off south through the woods at the east end of the Zonsche Forest, toward the canal. Also landing on the same DZ was B/506. Sergeant Herb Clark and his buddies had pooled money ($5,

each) in England until they had a pot of over $200, winner take all. The trooper with the first kill after landing would win the pot, but he had to have witnesses or proof of the kill.

Clark's group was on the ground, getting out of their chutes, when a lone German in the trees at the edge of the forest began firing at them with a rifle. Lieutenant Herb Viertel, Clark's platoon leader, was armed with a carbine, which fired erratically due to a worn sear. The weapon sometimes fired two or three shots in a burst with a single pull of the trigger. Viertel fired at the German and hit him through the chest with a two-round burst. He went over and removed the Soldbuch from the dead man's pocket; the two bullets had gone through the book right through the ID photo of the man's face. The dead German was a member of Flak Reg. 53, the same unit that manned the deadly 88's on the approach to the Son Bridge.

Chapter Four

Son To Eindhoven

When the 506 moved south from the DZ above Son, their objective was to capture the Son Bridge over the Wilhelmina Canal before the Germans could destroy it. The 1/506 went down Hell's Highway, passing through part of Son en route. John Lindsay, a bazookaman, knocked out an emplaced 88mm artillery position near the St. Aloysius Boys school. The 1/506 was paralleling second to the west, cutting south through the Zonsche Forest. As they neared the canal, mighty explosions thundered through the treetops, showering the troopers with deadly steel fragments. Don Burgett at first thought the men ahead had stepped on boobytraps, but several 88mm guns were positioned just north of the canal, west of the Son Bridge. Firing into the trees where 1/506 was approaching, they inflicted heavy casualties.

Captain Melvin Davis, CO of A/506, was hit by shell fragments. A medic knelt above him to give him aid. Two more shells banged-in, wounding the medic once and causing additional injuries to Davis. Turning to the medic, Davis said, "You better hurry, boy; they're *gaining* on you!"

Burgett recalled: "The shells kept hitting and slamming us, and they kept saying, "Keep going! Move forward; we've got to take the bridge!""

Lieutenant Bill Kennedy had jumped in with B/506. He recalled seeing Gen. Max Taylor near the canal. Taylor remarked to one of the 506th officers, "Now is the time for your men to be heroes." He was referring to a mad rush to capture the bridge intact.

Burgett and many others were up and running and Paul Carter and Earl Borchers had set up an LMG before becoming casualties of a nearby artillery explosion. Paul Carter was killed instantly. Borchers walked back past Burgett. Borchers was dazed and in shock and his buddies later learned that the blast had embedded the contents of his leg pocket into his upper leg. Among the items surgically removed, was a two-cell flashlight, potted meat in K-ration cans, chewing gum, and other odds and ends. His legs were shattered, yet he would rejoin

DZ C, 17 September 1944
A 506er in the foreground is gathering his equipment after landing. Scores of additional troopers can be seen dropping in the background. Al Krochka snapped this photo north of Son. *Krochka*

Fire on LZ W

Sergeant Ed Benecke (at left) stands beside the CG-4A Glider that carried No. 1 gun of A/377 to Holland on 17 September. Ed's nine-man crew were also aboard. The Germans had set fire to the grass of the peat bog on the LZ and succeeded in setting several gliders aflame. Parts of the 377 were forced to land by glider instead of parachute on this mission due to the loss of crews and guns on the Normandy misdrop. Only B/377 would parachute into Holland—two days later. *Benecke*

Victim of the Luftwaffe

As opposed to Normandy, the Luftwaffe made a strong showing in Holland during Market-Garden. The charred remains of a troop-carrier pilot lie beside his crashed plane on the Son DZ after a tragic attempted resupply drop. *Pistone* the 506th months later in Germany. According to Burgett, "In any other war in history, the man would've been sent home."

Burgett saw his buddy Phillips, but Phillips ran to the right while Burgett went to the left, near the North Brabant Sanitarium, a tuberculosis hospital. Shell blasts were raining down large shards of glass from the windows of the hospital. Burgett found another buddy dead there; his face had been sliced vertically in half, as if cut by a band saw.

Burgett paused to take the dead man's ammo, then joined in a charging group who were yelling, "Let's go!"

Burgett recalled:

We broke out of the woods and went running toward the guns. The only chance you've got is to take the people who are trying to kill you. If you stay there long enough, they're going to kill all of you. We ran toward three 88s in sandbagged encirclements on our side of the canal. One gun disappeared completely when the crew spiked it to pre-vent its capture. The blast also killed them. The sandbags, gun, and crew all disappeared. I ran toward one gun, which fired at us, flat trajectory. I felt the shell go past and heard it explode in the woods behind me. I went over the sandbags, and the crew immediately quit. [They] couldn't reload and had no arms except pistols. One guy fell on his back saying, "Nein, nein, nein," and he was crying like a baby. I came down with my bayonet to impale him, and he just put his arms up behind his head. I don't know how I stopped in time, but I did. This crew and the other one surrendered.

The troopers were almost to the bridge, when the Germans blew it. Burgett recalled:

I haven't been in too many explosions that were that big. It was a wooden bridge, and the whole bridge disappeared. Phillips was with me, and we hit the ground. I remember rolling over on my back. I looked up and saw what looked like a piece of a toothpick; I could see it twisting very

Glider Crash on LZ W
Two gliders collided about 35ft above the landing zone. One contained HQ personnel from the 501, including Tony Wysocki (who is still alive), and Lt. Lawrence Critchell, who wrote the 501 history *Four Stars of Hell*. In this photo, other paratroopers are working to free the survivors from the wreckage. *Krochka*

Commandeered Transport
Numerous carts and horse drawn wagons were appropri- ated by the troopers for moving heavy equipment off the DZ. *Simmons*

Wounded in the Jaw
Private Oscar Mendez had been wounded in the jaw while floating to the Eerde DZ in his parachute; he refused to be evacuated, and as evidenced by this photo, set out to gather equipment bundles from the DZ with a Dutch pedal cart. *Krochka*

slowly. I said, "Hey Phillips, look at that."

He said, "Yeah, that really went up high." It started coming back down, getting bigger and bigger. I started getting scared because it's coming right down and you don't know which way to run. But this thing was huge, and it didn't hit more than 40 or 50ft from us. You could feel the shock waves from it when it impaled right into the ground. It was about 2-1/2 ft square, about 30–40ft long.

Lieutenant Colonel LaPrade swam across the canal, and with the help of some engineers using planks, a crude footbridge was formed to move the 506 south toward their next objective: Eindhoven.

Eindhoven
The 1/ and 3/506 went halfway to Eindhoven along Hell's Highway, then stopped along both sides of the road for the night. Some additional Germans were killed in the vicinity of Bokt, and young Dutchmen quickly retrieved Mauser rifles to aid in the fighting. These Dutch resistance fighters tied a white armband around their upper arm, to signify that they were friendly to the Allied cause.
Don Burgett later said of the first night spent

Glidermen of C/401

A glider with a load of glider infantrymen of C/401 in England. This group flew to Holland on 18 September. At far left, standing, is Capt. Joe Brewster, S-2 of 1/401. Left to right (standing) are: T/Sgt. Grayson Davis, Sgt. George Naegle, unknown, Pfc. Ben Molinaro, and Pfc. Charlie Ratkic. Kneeling (left to right) are: Pfc. Frank Lombardino (KIA), Pfc. Ray Vigus, Pfc. Leonard Waddlington, and Pfc. George Miller (MIA). The tall officer standing at far right is Capt. Preston Towns, the company CO, who died of wounds near Bastogne in December 1944. The C-47 towing this glider was crippled by flak some 12–15 miles short of the LZ, so Captain Towns broke the plexiglass windshield out of the glider and cut off the tow rope with his trench knife. *US Army*

Blasted by a Bazooka

Somewhere in Holland, a member of HQ/326 AEB surveys a former German machine-gun nest. The gun and its crew were blasted into the ditch by a bazooka round. *Krochka*

A Souvenir
A trooper armed with a folding stock carbine retrieves a souvenir Luger pistol from the torn remains of the blasted German MG crew. *Krochka*

near Bokt, "We didn't dig holes that night, just lay down in the weeds and fell asleep. In the morning we got up like a buncha dogs, with dew dripping off our helmets."

The attack toward Eindhoven jumped off, with one platoon of A/506 staying behind to guard the temporary crossing at Son. The 3/506 led the way into Eindhoven. The British armor, which was supposed to be at the Son Bridge by 1800hr on 17 September, was still below Eindhoven, and the paratroopers would have to fight their way south to meet up with them.

Captain John Kiley, CO of I/506, was fatally shot by a sniper on the approach to Eindhoven. Members of H/506 and I/506 attacked, with H advancing through a cabbage patch to the edge of town. Lt. Rudolph Bolte was killed in that area, along with Jon Hanson. Charlie Kier was shot through the chest while going through a gate.

Hank DiCarlo considered James Tarquini to be one of the best combat men in H/506. He saw Tarquini crash through a plate-glass window, circle through a building, and come up from behind to knock out an MG position. Sgt. Frank Padisak was also instrumental in the fighting.

Coming into Eindhoven from the north, S/Sgt. Jerry Beam and Lt. Charles Santasiero engaged an 88mm gun position but were halted. The 2/506 entered town from the east. Rifle grenadiers from F/506, including Robert Sherwood and Homer Smith, joined S/Sgt. John H. Taylor and others in knocking out two 88's from the flank.

It was surmised that much of the German garrison had left Eindhoven to join the big fight at Best.

Clearing out high rise buildings was a new experience to these paratroopers who were experienced mainly in hedgerow fighting. The giant Phillips Electric building was searched floor by floor by members of H/506. A/506 men were assigned several high-rise buildings and rode by elevator car to the top of each. The troopers operating the elevator would say, "Floor please," and take them up. Exiting at the top, they worked their way down, checking each office, but finding no Germans.

Members of H/506 entered a park within Eindhoven and encountered an outhouse. Luther Myers entered for some privacy, but the Germans had booby-trapped the toilet. When Myers pulled the handle to flush the toilet, the outhouse exploded, miraculously leaving him seated on the throne, unharmed. DiCarlo recalled seeing him holding the

Guards Armored Division
Commonwealth troops of the Guards Armored Div. pause along Hell's Highway to mingle with Dutch civilians. *Dutch photo via Hopke*

handle with his pants around his ankles, surrounded by smoke.

In the afternoon, British scout vehicles entered Eindhoven and proceeded north toward Son. Two of them would contact Lieutenant Wierzbowski's H/502 platoon near Best. The British armor would reach Son and erect a Bailey Bridge over the Wilhelmina Canal by 0600hr on 19 September. By then, the operation was already seriously behind schedule.

Massive celebrations with the civilian populace ensued, and sandwiches, beer and fruit were lavished upon the liberators. Some would spend the night in town while others pulled security on the east and west outskirts, and some 506ers joined British tanks in a push toward Nunen, Holland, well to the east. An air raid hit Eindhoven that night with the Luftwaffe making the first of increasingly strong bombings.

Don Burgett recalled that some young Dutch girls brought food and blankets out to the US foxhole line that night. They walked along until they saw a trooper who looked attractive to them, then got into the foxhole and spent the night.

Panther Hunters
Paratroopers pose a top a KO'd Mk V Panther tank. *Dovholuk*

27

HQ Troops
Ralph Cross and Paul Teator stand in front of the church in Son, Holland. The first divisional CP of the 101st in Holland was in a school contiguous to this church. *Teator*

Galla and Palmieri
Members of division HQ (G-3) pose near Son. Shown are M/Sgt. George Galla and "Booby-Trap" Palmieri. *Teator*

One of the 88mm guns stationed in Son. It is believed that this one was KO'd by John Lindsey of the 506 with a bazooka round. *US Army*

Back To Son

On 20 September, the Germans made a concerted counterattack on Son, coming along the south side of the canal from the east. The 1/506 was rushed north to assist elements of the 326 and HQ/101 personnel in repulsing the attacks. The Germans were using Panther tanks, and Col. Ned Moore succeeded in hitting one with a bazooka. The German unit had recently arrived from a quiet sector and was reluctant to pursue its attack with a total effort. They did manage to kill a number of 506ers who were dug-in along the dike.

The 1/327, as well as elements of the 81 joined the fight, and division headquarters was moved north to the Henkenshage Castle at St. Oedenrode.

Fresh Milk

Fresh milk, a treat rarely seen by the WWII paratrooper, is enjoyed by an unknown 506er in Eindhoven. *Dutch*

Airborne Friends

D/506 Machine-Gunners
Two D/506 machine-gunners in Eindhoven. Frank Anness supplied this photo, although he doesn't remember the troopers' names. One of the gunners said he was so sick of cleaning the machine gun that he was going to take one home after the war and leave it in his garden in all kinds of weather, just to watch it get dirty and rusty. *Anness*

Collaborators
In Eindhoven, Dutch girls who had slept with German soldiers had their hair shorn off in public as a form of retribution. They were then banished from their hometown. The men labeled as collaborators faced a worse fate—prompt trials, usually followed by summary execution. *Musura*

Chapter Five

Best and St. Oedenrode

The village of Best, Holland, lies almost 4mi west of Hell's Highway, and like Son, is situated near the Wilhelmina Canal. Upon landing on the 17th, it was learned that the two bridges near the main Son Bridge had been destroyed by the Germans shortly before the jump. When the main Son Bridge was destroyed in the faces of approaching paratroopers, it seemed like a good idea to General Taylor to send a force west to try and capture the alternate bridge over the canal south of Best. This was initially deemed a mission suited to a company, so H/502 was detached from 3/502 to capture and hold the bridge—if it was still intact.

Charlie Company at St. Oedenrode

The 1/502, under Lt. Col. Pat Cassidy was sent north to capture St. Oedenrode. Company C, under Capt. Fred Hancock led off, and after a brief but brisk skirmish, the defenders were killed or driven off.

The next two days in that sector were relatively quiet, and some of Hancock's men published a mimeographed one-page daily newsletter for the local troops, entitled the *Charlie Chronicle.* On 17–18 September things were so slow for C/502 that the first edition of the *Chronicle* said:

This headquarters is contemplating laying airstrips to get back out. There doesn't seem to be enough action here for tough Airborne men. So far on this cakewalk old Charlie has done pretty good . . . Some time this PM Maxwell was seen talking to Pat at a prominent road junction—maybe we will

get another bite of those Germans. I know you are disappointed with the slight action we have seen so far, but Germany hasn't capitulated yet.

Foxhole Correspondents
Two members of the 502 in a foxhole near Best. One is reading an old letter from home as the other writes a letter home. Note they are both on guard for the enemy at the same time; one holds his carbine and the other a .45 pistol. *Swartz*

Smit Saves His Buddies
Lieutenant Morton J. Smit, a platoon leader with C/502, was wounded in the intense fighting near St. Odenrode on 19 September 1944. An exchange of hand grenades and small-arms fire took place at very short range. Smit, lying behind a hedge, suddenly saw a German concussion grenade sail in. The sputtering grenade landed quite close to Smit, and he felt there was not enough time to throw it back. Smit quickly decided to smother the blast effects of the grenade by placing his steel helmet over it and lying on it. Smit thus absorbed much of the blast, saving his nearby comrades from injury. The grenade blast broke Smit's arm in several places and shattered his left hip, which has required a number of surgeries to correct since the war. This photo was taken as Smit was about to be evacuated to a field hospital. He is smiling because he is happy to be alive and because he was feeling the effects of morphine. Captain Fred Hancock, Smit's CO, snapped this photo. *Smit*

In the second edition, the situation was already rapidly changing:

> Jerry tossed a few kitchen sinks over here in the early morning hours but had the wrong range. Patrols were sent out from the 3rd Platoon to try and locate their guns but had very little success. However, I believe from the sound of their muzzle blasts, the guns were sitting in behind our lines and the patrols were out to their front. Unconfirmed report that Jerry is approaching our positions from four different directions and so many that we couldn't count them with an adding machine. The Dutch are just trying to be helpful when they give you these reports, but try to get some confirmation of them before sending them in—I can't sleep nights with such reports. Those five hundred Krauts just up the road have increased to eight hundred. Should we send the British up there or write home and tell them to sell the outhouse?

(*Charlie Chronicles* provided courtesy of Fred Hancock.)

Despite the dire forecast, the situation in St. Oedenrode would never approach the magnitude of the fighting near Best. But aggressive patrols went out continuously, like spokes of a wheel, mostly to the west of the town. The C/502, sometimes supported by a tank from the Irish Guards, pushed repeatedly northwest along the road to Schijndel. The B/502, went roughly toward Olland, to the west, while A/502 probed toward the southwest in the direction of Donderdonk.

Despite the smaller number of casualties near St. Oedenrode, the local casualties were adding-up and the small actions were close-up and furious.

Jay Nichols of B/502 recalled losing his captain, "Buck" Rogers, wounded and evacuated, as well as Pvt. Redmond Wells, KIA. Capt. Fred Hancock, C/502 CO, caught a Schmeisser slug through the chest. Spitting blood, he walked a quarter-mile back to the aid station. Although evacuated from Holland, Fred would return to the 502 in a few months.

A Gathering Storm At Best

On 17 September, Capt. Bob Jones had led his H/502 to the west edge of the Zonsche Forest. One platoon, under Lieutenant Harper, was sent west to try to enter the town of Best. The platoon came under fire and was pinned down. During a lull in the shooting, a German truck convoy drove down the road between the two sides, seemingly unaware of the situation. Someone shot the motorcyclist who was leading the truck convoy, and the trucks stopped, disgorging dozens of German infantrymen, who joined the battle.

Another H/502 platoon, under Lieutenant Duffy, had probed south through the forest but was also halted and driven back. The company was alone on the west edge of the airborne bridgehead, and the enemy concentrated all the fury of their artillery on that section of the woods. Throughout the night, tree-bursts rained steel down into foxholes, and American casualties multiplied.

On the first evening, a platoon under leadership of Lt. Ed Wierzbowski had set off to the south, determined to seize and hold the bridge over the Wilhelmina Canal south of Best. With that platoon was part of Lt. James E. Watson's 3rd Platoon of C/326. This group broke out of the woods some 500yd east of the bridge and following the slippery embankment parallel to the canal, worked slowly west toward the bridge. The group paused only 30yd short of the bridge, which was still intact, but guarded by two German sentries.

At this time (according to S.L.A. Marshall), the American group numbered 18 men from H/502 and 26 from the 326. One of the scouts, Joe Eugene Mann, went forward to the bridge, at a crawl, with Lieutenant Wierzbowski. The duo was nearly spotted by one of the sentries and had to lie still for over a half hour, during which the larger group behind them was wondering what to do. Finally, a mixed group of engineers and H/502 men stood up and ran for the rear.

Mann and Wierzbowski used this confusion to jump up and re-join the group at the base of the embankment. Having decided to stay, the stage was now set for a last-stand battle by Wierzbowski's group. Any thought he might have held of capturing the bridge was soon eroded by the ever growing numbers of German troops entering the area. But the fighting spirit of this group was not diminished. Vincent Laino of the engineers was a machine-gunner. He had his gun and 500 rounds of ammunition.

Tree of Life
In September 1994, former 326th AEB machine-gunner Bob Granche returned to this spot in Holland for the first time since WWII, 50 years after this oak tree shielded him from the blast of a German grenade. Before returning to Holland, he had not attended reunions or talked about this incident because his citation says he killed a Dutch civilian who was mixed in with the Germans that night. Talking to Dutchman M. Sanders in 1994, Granche learned that the man in civilian clothes was a German soldier who had gotten fed-up with the war and had begged the clothes from Sanders so he could desert to Germany. *Granche*

There was also a bazooka with five rounds and a 60mm mortar with six rounds.

It rained hard during the night, and Wierzbowski's group had been located by the Germans. It was just a matter of time before they would close-in to finish the group off.

At 1100hr on the morning of the 18th, the Germans detonated the bridge over the canal south of Best. There was no way for Wierzbowski's group to

Airborne Artillerymen
New arrivals—possibly members of the 377—greet Dutch kids in St. Oedenrode circa 19 September 1944. Note that the trooper at left is equipped with a 1928A1 Tommygun and has acquired an A-2 leather flight jacket, which is tied around his neck by the sleeves. *Nichols*

Where'd You Get that Jeep?
Troopers lucky enough to swipe a jeep usually beat the numbers off the front fender and sometimes christened the vehicle with a new name. This jeep was acquired by the 506's regimental S-2 section, and one of them is applying the new name. *Palys*

KO'd Tank
Knocked-out British tank on Hells Highway; the crew is buried alongside. *Krochka*

communicate this fact to their company or battalion HQ.

The Death of Lt. Col. Cole

Back at H/502, Captain Jones had pulled his troops deeper in to the woods to try to avoid some of the heavy mortar and artillery shelling which was decimating his men. Lieutenant Colonel Cole's position was also under heavy fire, and he had called for air support. P-47 fighters were to bomb and strafe the nearby woods where Germans were firing on his battalion. A shell killed T/5 Robert Doran, Cole's radio operator, and the first P-47's to arrive strafed Cole's positions by mistake. Just as Cole was about to run into the open to readjust the aircraft recognition panels in front of his positions, Sgt. Graham Armstrong arrived with an S-2 patrol. Armstrong told Cole that Colonel Michaelis wanted to know whether the bridge over the canal had been captured.

"Screw the bridge!," said Cole, who was preoccupied with the immediate problem of friendly planes attacking his men. Cole ran out into the field and was shot through the head. He died instantly. Bob Cole was thereby robbed of the honor of receiving his Medal of Honor. It would be awarded a few months later for the bayonet charge he had led, back in Normandy.

Joe Mann Sacrifices Himself for His Buddies

After the bridge was blown, Mann and Hoyle had moved the bazooka to a mound west of the platoon position and fired at a German ammo dump. The second round blew it up. Six Germans attacked their position from the north. Mann and Hoyle were able to shoot them all, but the attackers succeeded in wounding Mann in both shoulders. Hoyle then used the bazooka to destroy an 88mm gun position 150yd away.

Wounded from this fight were being placed in a separate hole from the men still fighting. Joe Mann received two more wounds, and his arms were both placed in slings, but he refused to join the wounded, begging to remain with the men still fighting.

During that night, two British recon cars appeared across the canal and a platoon from D/502

Tea Time
Divisional photographer Albert A. Krochka paused to drink tea with some battle-weary Brits from the Guards Armored Div. on Hell's Highway, September 1944. *Krochka*

POWS, 18 September 1944
Members of C/502 outside St. Oedenrode with German prisoners. *Smit*

joined Wierzbowski's group, but both units pulled out before the Germans counterattacked the next morning.

On the misty morning on the 19th, Wierzbowski saw a German officer leading a file of men toward his position. He yelled to Betrus, who tossed a grenade. But German grenades were already sailing in. A chaotic flurry of activity began, with paratroopers tossing out live grenades and firing furiously at available targets.

Lawrence Koller was shot through the head, and Laino was taking a heavy toll of the attackers with his LMG. A German ran up from the right, firing a sweeping burst with a Schmeisser at a downward angle toward Laino's head. A 9mm slug imbedded in Laino's jaw, but he lifted the LMG, swinging it around and firing a long burst. He saw several tracers pass through the German before the enemy hit the ground. A German grenade flew in, and Laino grabbed it, throwing it back just before it exploded. The blast took out one eye and blinded Laino in the other. He called for a medic, but Orvac, the only available aidman was busy working on Koller.

Yet another grenade thumped on the ground behind Joe Mann. Sitting with both arms in slings, he was unable to toss it out. He yelled, "Grenade! I'm taking this one!" He laid back on the explosive just as it detonated. The concussion lifted him, and shrapnel hit several others in the hole. But Mann's sacrifice had saved their lives. He reportedly said,

German Tankette
A German tankette KO'd by fire from British Typhoon fighter plane near St. Oedenrode. The troopers aboard it are from 1st Platoon of C/326. *Crilley*

"My back is gone," then died without a moan. A posthumous award of the Medal of Honor was made.

Soon after the explosion that took Mann's life, the group capitulated. They were out of grenades and low on ammo. The survivors were marched north to a field hospital near Best. Later that day, they grabbed weapons when the Germans weren't paying attention, captured the hospital, and returned to US lines to fight again. (Note: This account differs in detail from that given by S.L.A. Marshall, but it is based on the testimony of Vincent Laino,

A British-made Cromwell tank pauses in St. Oedenrode along Hell's Highway. *Musura*

Halftrack Ambulances
Halftracks pressed into medical evacuation service in the vicinity of St. Oedenrode. *Crilley*

who described the experience to Bob Granche in a hospital ward soon after the events took place. Granche related the story to the author.)

Bob Granche's Roadblock

Like other men in C/326's 3rd Platoon, Bob Granche (pronounced *Granchee*) was tall. He didn't relish combat, but like his fellow machine-gunner Vince Laino, he took pride in outperforming his opponents. Granche liked the A-6 LMG with bipod and shoulder stock and carried the weapon, along with a carbine, in Holland.

On the night of September 18–19, shortly before midnight, Granche was selected to lead a three-man patrol north to where a path formed a T with the Son–Best road. Near there, he was to establish a roadblock. Starting out along the path with two other troopers, Granche reached his objective around 2400hr. The American trio walked right up to three Germans who were standing there in the dark. The Germans didn't realize the approaching troops were Americans until Granche sprayed some bullets at them from his carbine. He succeeded in dropping two of them.

Working quickly, Granche led his buddies east along the tree-lined road for about 100yd, then selected a tall oak tree on the north shoulder to blast with C-2. Affixing the charge, he detonated it, felling the tree across the road. He then dragged the two dead Germans to a sitting position, and propped them up with their backs to the tree, facing toward Best. He also put their helmets on them.

Granche placed his LMG in the north ditch about 20ft west of the felled tree. Granche and friends were brought under fire within 10min by German infantry. At a range of less than 50ft, bul-

Armored Casualty
Another German armored casualty along Hell's Highway was this StuGIII, equipped with a short-barreled 75mm main battery. Vehicles of this type were not frequently seen by 1944. *Benecke*

Ambushed and Decimated
Part of the British column on Hell's Highway, ambushed and decimated on 24 September near Koevering. The long column of British supply trucks was caught on an open stretch of Hell's Highway north of St. Oedenrode and wiped out. A combination of 40mm cannon fire and small arms from the German Jungwirth Bn. laid waste to the convoy, and an estimated 300 British soldiers were killed. *Krochka*

lets flew across the road fast and furious. Granche and friends had several grenades apiece. They threw all of them across the road and fired their weapons. Bob burned through 500 rounds of LMG ammo. There was a brief lull in the fighting for a couple minutes.

A group of 14 additional German troops, including a man dressed in civilian clothes, exited a house 100yd west of the roadblock and joined the men in the south ditch. Firing resumed. A German grenade sailed across the road, thumping Granche in the chest. He reached down feeling in the dark for the deadly object. Seconds elapsed, and Granche had not found it. He dove for cover behind a large oak tree, just as the grenade detonated. The tree saved Granche's life, but one of his feet was mangled by the blast. The other troopers fled east and north, leaving the position.

Despite his painful wound, Granche crawled back into position behind his LMG. Several Germans arose from the ditch across the road and began walking toward his position. Evidently, they assumed the grenade had killed him.

Granche swept them all down with a burst of fire.

Things got quiet, and Granche realized that all the enemy soldiers across the road had been killed.

He crawled back to the T junction, then made his way south for a distance of 300yd to inform his commander that the roadblock was no longer manned. A patrol was sent back to the spot, guided by Granche. An officer liked Bob's touch of propping the dead Germans against the fallen tree. A few more were added, and Granche later received the Silver Star for this action.

As mentioned in the previous chapter, even the German garrison in Eindhoven had been diverted to the area near Best, to participate in the growing conflict there.

The 2/502 left their reserve position near Wolfswinkel on the 18th and moved west to join the battle at Best also.

"I *Told* You Guys Not To Go In That Barn!"

Corporal Joe Pistone was with his platoon leader, Lt. Robert Banker, during the move to Best. Pistone's 8–10-man group began to fall behind the company advance when his group came under fire and their horse-drawn supply came under fire.

They moved on into the hamlet of Molenkampen. There in a bunker behind a farmhouse, they found 30 Dutch civilians hiding from the firing.

As dusk began to settle in, Pistone looked for a place to spend the night. He moved several hundred

Military Intelligence
Harry Silver, S-2 in the 502, examines a KO'd German self-propelled gun on Hell's Highway. *Pangerl*

yards east, to a house on the edge of the DZ. Parachutes were strewn all over the field, as were a number of gliders. The nearby farmhouse had a barn attached, and in it were a number of wounded with attending medics and the 502's chaplains, Raymond Hall (Protestant), and Father Andrejewski. Pistone found a parachute canopy and decided to bed down for the night in a ditch near the farmhouse. His men complained that they were cold and wanted to go into the barn for warmth.

"That's the first place the Germans are going to look," Pistone warned them. "For Chrissake, stay out here!" The men drifted away in the darkness and later did go into the barn.

Pistone was comfortably wrapped in his parachute canopy when he was awakened by some "loud stage whispers," around 0100hr. He heard equipment clanking and then one shot was fired near the barn. About 35 American troops were in the barn. A voice shouted in English, "Either you surrender, or we'll burn the building down!"

Many of the troops in the barn had removed their boots, and they filed out and marched away into captivity in their stocking feet. This group would remain captive for the duration of the war. Pistone was in the ditch, "really scared," as the group walked away in the darkness. He was afraid

to shoot because he couldn't distinguish friend from enemy in the darkness. Other German troops crossed the ditch to search some of the gliders, their boots thumping the embankment of the ditch, right beside Pistone's head.

After everything quieted down, Pistone spent a scary night alone in the ditch. At dawn he approached the barn and encountered Lou Zotti of HQ/2 502. Zotti had spent the night on the opposite side of the building.

"What happened?," said Zotti.

"My whole squad is missing," said Pistone.

As they stood talking, Father Andrejewski came out of the barn. He had hidden deep in the hayloft and had evaded capture.

Sergeant Earl Cox, F/502's operations sergeant made an entry in his journal that day, listing some of the men who were missing as a result of the above described incident: Silfies, Bolkus, Crosby, Dellande, Franklin, Gallagher, Milineczenko, Smith, Turner, Weston, Fellers, Moore, and Wilson.

Pistone proceed on to rejoin F/502 near Best. He could hear the fierce fighting from a distance, and he located Lieutenant Banker. Banker was infuriated and wanted to know where Pistone and his squad had been. Pistone was finally able to calm Banker down and relate the story.

Some members of Pistone's squad were liberated before VE-day and came to visit the 101st before returning to the States. Joe's first words upon seeing them again were:

"I *told* you guys not to go in that barn!"

As the fight for Best continued, German troops kept pouring in. They were members of the Fifteenth Army who had been diverted from their trip to the German border to join the fight, as well as units transported from afar to aid in the fighting.

British tanks reinforced 2/ and 3/502 on the 19th. In a drive along the west edge of the Zonsche Forest, a climax of sorts ended the first phase of fighting there. Over 1,100 prisoners were rounded-up and marched east, away from the fighting. Even so, the Germans continued to hold the town of Best itself for many weeks to come.

Private Sterno's Second Odyssey

Private Bernard Sterno was a fortunate survivor of Cole's immortal bayonet charge at the north edge of Carentan. A member of H/502, Sterno was wounded on four separate occasions on that single afternoon of 10 June 1944. His ordeal has been well-documented in several history books. Bernard was still hospitalized for his multiple wounds in England when he heard news of the Market-Garden invasion on the radio. Sterno left the hospital and headed for his old base camp to see about catching a plane to Holland to join his buddies. Thus began Sterno's second, lesser-known odyssey, as told in his own words:

The same self-propelled gun was snapped in profile by S/Sgt. Ed Benecke of A/377. Ed Says this was along Hell's Highway between Koevering and Veghel. *Benecke*

A trooper named Bluett from A Company got out of the hospital the same day as me, 17 September, a Sunday. We said, "Darn it, we missed the invasion." We made our way back to Chilton Foliat to our base camp, near Hungerford. I wanted to catch a plane ride over to Holland so I could jump in and rejoin my outfit. I heard the voice of my sergeant, J. B. Cooper, and didn't want him to see me (I knew if he found out about my plan he would put me on restriction or something). We heard that Sergeant Kremer and someone else were going to London to try to catch a boat ride to the continent. We learned that resupply planes were taking off daily from Ramsbury. There was a quonset hut full of weapons, ammunition and grenades, so we equipped ourselves and slept that night away from Cooper and the old barracks. We went to the airfield at Ramsbury and approached a C-47 crew that was preparing to load up equipment for a resupply mission.

We walked over like we belonged there.

"Which one of these damned planes are we supposed to be on?" I asked.

"What do you mean?"

"We're supposed to get combat jumpmaster experience on these darned things."

Some young flight engineer or something, said, "I could sure use some help on my plane."

"Doesn't matter which one of 'em I'm on, as long as I'm on one of 'em."

"I'll get you some parachutes and flak jackets."

A little while later, a jeep pulled up with two white canopied pilot type parachutes and two flak vests.

We sat there about an hour or two before take-off. The crew chief was looking at us and said, "I don't know about you guys. I'm kind of leery that you have *plans* of some kind."

He didn't say anymore. We got on the plane and he said, "We're going to take a lot of flak when

The Supa Dupa Paratrooper
Mike Musura took many of the photos in this book as one of the 101st's divisional photographers.

we drop this off, when we make our turn to come back; before we get there we'll get a lot of flak."

Beautiful sunshiney day, I was lyin' on the floor, looking out the door of the plane.

We got to the drop zone and threw the bundles out. Bluett, the guy who was with me got sick; he was throwing-up in his helmet. I told him "You'd better not jump," and he didn't.

We were looking down and I said "Where do you think we're at?"

The crew chief pointed down at Hell's Highway, which was lined with vehicles and said, "I

don't know, but that's the British supply line there." I stood in the door and some impulse hit me, and I just dove out.

Instead of the three-thousand count, I did a five-thousand count, and pulled the ripcord.

Coming down, I could see people coming from all around—some in the distance looked like Germans, some looked like civilians.

I landed, dropped the ripcord handle, and two 12-year-olds walked up with their hands out. We shook hands. I handed one of 'em my carbine while I unfastened my harness, then took it back. They picked the chute up and took it away. So all these other people from the village were there. Girls were hugging me, and an older man drove up on a bicycle, all excited.

He got me on the back of that bicycle and started riding me toward his village. He got tired, stopped to wipe the sweat off. He made me take off my helmet, and I held it low with my carbine. I had nice long flowing blond hair then. We went past a hedge, and he waved, and I waved . . . were those Germans? Can't be.

We got in the village. This priest came out and hugged me. This lady about 35-years-old walked right down the street toward me.

"Are you American or English?" she asked.

"I'm American."

"We must get you out of here—Germans everywhere," she said in perfect English.

She asked if I would visit this old man who was dying, who hadn't seen an American in five years. I said, "Certainly." I went in the building. She translated, and I shook hands with him. They poured me a drink, and I drank it. A Dutch Underground man wearing an orange armband and rifle arrived. They got me a girl's bicycle. The Underground man rode ahead of me. At each curve, he would stop like a scout, then motion me on.

We got to the main road, and a couple heads bobbed up behind an MG, which was pointed right at us.

"Yank," they said, "there's Jerries over there." I asked them about the 101st.

"Oh, your blokes are down that way," they said. I pedaled up along all these English trucks which were stalled on the highway.

Coincidentally, some regimental medics of the 502 came up, and one guy recognized me. They gave me a ride down to the regimental area, and I slept that night on a stretcher.

In the morning I asked where was third battalion as I walked along past all these MG and rifle positions. I found the H Company CP in this farm building by a large pile of hay. They were heating-up coffee and stuff for breakfast. When I walked in, they all looked shocked and surprised. I walked up to 1st Sgt. Harry Bush and said, "I want to get on the morning report."

"Good, what's your rank now?"

"I'm a buck private. I'm AWOL. I just took one of the Air Corps' parachutes."

"Don't worry about that, they're laying all over the country here."

First Sergeant Bush promoted me to buck sergeant on the spot; they needed squad leaders because of all the casualties. The guys I knew were all around talking to me. One guy said "We killed a lot of Germans." About half our guys were wounded or dead. Weren't too many left.

They gave me some K-rations and grenades, and I swapped my carbine to somebody for a grease gun.

The next morning was September 21 and we moved out. I was walking with Jack Dunwoodie about 3:00 or 4:00 in the afternoon, when someone told me to take the point and go pick up some wounded Germans. I started walking down this road, and where it curved, I never saw so many Germans in my life. I raised the grease gun overhead with both hands to signal those behind me the enemy was in sight. The large group walking toward me hadn't spotted me when I dove in the ditch for cover. But at the same time, a group across the field opened fire on me. I was wondering why my people didn't come to help me. Maybe they were thinking I got riddled or killed. Every time I raised up, a bullet would hit near me. So there was a brick building across the road from me, and I saw two of them walking beside that building. I know now why that guy swapped me the grease gun. I fired three shots, knocked that one German down, and the other one screamed; he went crawling through the bushes. I pulled the bolt and shot at him several times. Whether it killed him or not I don't know—I never heard any more from him anyway. So the ones in front, they didn't see me yet. They kept getting closer and closer. I didn't know what I'm gonna do. One raised up, saw me, ducked

back down, I said "Oh, hell." I heard a noise. *Chic*, like that. I knew what it was—the cord being pulled on a potato-masher grenade. I looked up and there it was coming. I put my head between my knees, crumpled down, and it went off. That was almost as bad as when that shell hit near me in Normandy. It blew my helmet off . . . my eyes, I couldn't see nothing, thought I was blind. I heard a voice: "Kommen, kommen, kommen." I rubbed my eyes; I could see a blur. Finally, after getting tears out of my eyes to where I could see, there was a German squatting there, with a rifle pointed at me. So I got up and walked toward him. He just put his rifle on his shoulder and told me to follow him. I know why he wasn't worried about me because that whole ditch, all the way down, was loaded with Germans.

He stopped, pulled an apple off the tree, and I stopped, pulled me one off, and we got to the German first-aid station there. The German officer there could speak English fluently. They treated me real nice there. I asked for some water, he said "The water is no good, could you drink some milk?" I said, "Sure"

I found out after the war that when I didn't come back some of the guys said, "He's in trouble; let's go get him!" But some lieutenant said, "No, we gotta keep going."

Although Sterno escaped German captivity twice, he was destined to spend most of the duration of WWII as a POW in German captivity. He had a remarkable series of adventures that would require a separate book to tell. He jumped out of a boxcar on a moving train for his first escape, evading the Germans for six days before being recaptured.

This remarkably courageous trooper was eventually liberated by the Russian Army. He was discharged after VE-day. Two and a half years later, he re-enlisted and served an entire career in the military.

Two Tanks in One Day

Lieutenant Kenneth Shaw (later KIA at Bastogne) of the 377 got word one afternoon that German tanks were approaching on a sunken lane east of Hell's Highway. He went into the woods overlooking the lane from the south with Sgt. Art Parker acting as bazookaman, and two machine-gunners. A line of Panther tanks appeared, with infantry riding atop them. The machine-gunners dusted off the infantry as Parker fired his first rocket down against the lead tank. The rocket bounced off. The second round stopped the tank, halting the tank column. Art fired into the second tank, also disabling it. The rest of the German armor was forced to halt the attack and back all the way to their line of departure.

Panzer Sgt. Richard Durig
German Panzer Sgt. Richard Durig, a veteran of the 33rd Panzer Reg., 9th Panzer Div. Entries in his Soldbuch indicate that he had been wounded at Kursk, suffered a nervous breakdown in January 1944, and survived the Falaise Pocket in Normandy. He died along Hell's Highway in September 1944. (See the letter from Art Parker in the text.)

Hordes of POWs
By 20 September, the 502 had captured over 2,000 prisoners from the German Fifteenth Army in the Best-St. Oedenrode area. Hordes of POWs were marched to waiting trucks. The prisoners were driven south, transferred to trains, then boarded ships that took them to the US. A trooper named Olsen from G/502 accompanied a large group of POWs all the way back to the US—naturally, without authorization. *Musura*

Two tanks in one day—not bad for a survey and instrument man from the field artillery. Art was awarded the Silver Star for this action, but always regretted that the lieutenant and machine-gunners didn't get any credit.

The Man in Black

The next day, not far away, German infantry attacked a portion of the highway held by 1/506. The 75mm cannons of the 377 also joined in repulsing them. Art Parker noticed that the Germans were hanging-back in their advance due to the bursting 75mm shells. A panzer corporal dressed in a black uniform was trying to drive the infantry forward and even shot several of his own men with a machine pistol when they hesitated to advance. The man in black was later identified as Richard Durig

of the 33rd Panzer Reg. He himself was wounded, and the surviving Germans rushed forward with their hands high to surrender. A group of troopers walked out to apprehend the man in black, but he fought kicked and cursed them. He resisted being searched but was dragged back in the line at the highway.

The other Germans seemed more scared of him than they were of their captors. Durig cursed and spit at them and tried to incite them to overpower their captors. A 506er finally gave Durig a pistol shot to the head, which shut him up for good.

Parker kept Durig's bloody Soldbuch, which revealed that Durig had been wounded at Kursk, Russia, the previous fall.

Parker later wrote:

We shook Durig down, and I kept the paybook to show the guys back at headquarters. The Germans pulled off his I.D. tag and threw it in the woods. They didn't want to leave his body in the ditch where it would be found, so they threw it down an open well in front of a farmhouse. His bones are probably still down there. I think the reason the captured Germans wanted to get rid of his body was they still thought the German Army would push us out of Holland and his body would be found with a bullet in the head, and they would be blamed.

Chapter Six

Eerde-Schijndel

The small village of Eerde lies southwest of Veghel, and the loamy plowed fields in between became DZ A for 2/ and 3/501.

The 2/501 would remain mostly in and around Veghel during the first two weeks of the campaign while 3/501 moved immediately to occupy Eerde and outpost the highway to St. Oedenrode. The 1/501 would act as a mobile force, circulating in many villages north and west of Veghel.

A large windmill marked the north end of town, and a church with a sizable marble statue of Christ in front stands in the center of town. German forces moving toward Hell's Highway from the west soon recognized the strategic importance of Eerde and as a result, the tiny village became an important focal point of the fighting.

In the early fighting, 3/501 was in and out of Eerde, and 1/501 took up positions near the railroad track north of town, where tall sand dunes dotted the landscape. The dunes were visible both from the church steeple in town and from the large windmill. On 24 September, a German attack supported by tanks attempted to enter Eerde from the dunes and A/501 went into the dunes to clear them in face-to-face fighting. This encounter has been well-documented in both the regimental and divisional histories.

"Old Glory" and the Sand Dunes

One of the enduring folk legends of the town concerns the use of the steeple of the church to observe artillery fire into the dunes.

After a forward observer from the 907 refused to mount the steeple due to the hazards of German artillery, Lt. Harry Howard of 1/501 ascended to observe for the artillery. Frank Carpenter of C/501 described what happened next:

> The Germans started the day off by firing down on us from the high ground, with the notion of taking Eerde. I remember looking back on the village shortly after the fight started and saw someone climbing the church spire and attaching the American flag to a pole on top of it. The Germans, taking issue with this show of impudence, pulled up a tank

Troopers of 3/501 enter Eerde. *Krochka*

Elite Intelligence Unit
An S-2 patrol from HQ/501 is about to depart on a reconnaissance mission from Eerde, Holland, late September 1944. The trooper at far left with the BAR is Robert Nicolai, one of Col. Howard Johnson's bodyguards. Second from left with Tommygun is Sgt. Eugene Amburgey. The oil-cloth American-flag invasion arm brassard is visible on both of these men. In the center of the photo is Dick "Smokey" Ladman, and behind Ladman, holding a radio, is David Smith. The staff sergeant is John F. Tiller. Colonel Johnson considered his regimental S-2 platoon an elite corps, and they would soon win international fame for conducting the Incredible Patrol in October 1944 on the Island. *Canfield*

and blew down the top of the church, flag, pole, and all. Shortly thereafter, there again was the flag waving from the topmost point—and again it was blown down. All through the morning this act was repeated, with neither the German tank crew or the trooper [Lieutenant Howard] giving up. A platoon of British tankers were sent up to help us take the dunes, but the German tanker knocked them all out before they got off a shot. Shortly, we got word to take the dunes, and we did. I still remember looking back at the village, from the dunes this time, and seeing "Old Glory" waving from the top-most point of what was left of the church spire. It was a sight I will never forget as long as I live. Oh yes, we got the German tank that night with a WP barrage from division artillery.

(Harry Howard was a career soldier who died in the 1970s. His heroic defiance of the Germans provided great inspiration both to his comrades and the Dutch onlookers. He has become one of the legendary figures of the WWII 101st.)

The Night Attack on Schijndel

The success of Lt. Col. Harry Kinnard's sweep in the Heewijk-Dinter area had convinced Col. Howard Johnson of the need to disrupt German staging areas west of Veghel before organized attacks could be mounted. Dutch resistance fighters had brought word that the Germans were massing troops in Schijndel, west of Eerde, and Johnson ordered 1/ and 3/501 to attack that village on the night of 21–22 September, with short notice and no prior reconnaissance. Lieutenant Colonel Julian Ewell of 3/501 was so agitated by the order that he wanted to "turn-in my soldier suit." Attempts to reach the colonel by radio were unsuccessful, and the attack jumped off as ordered, with 1/501 coming into town from the east and drawing the first enemy fire. A German mobile flak wagon was one of the worst aspects of enemy fire and after bedeviling 1/501, the vehicle moved around to fire at 3/501.

Ewell's battalion crossed the railroad tracks and came at Schijndel from the southeast, skirting the towns of Hoeven and Berg en route.

Melton "Tex" McMorries of G/501 described the Schijndel attack as follows:

> I don't know the name, but this village [Hoeven] was occupied by civilians, and we could plainly hear the weird sounds of many voices. These voices picked up, and all the villagers joined from one length to the end, which I suppose was prayers. Of course this automatically pointed out that somewhere ahead of us lay the enemy.

> First Battalion to our right was the lead attack battalion, because although enemy MG fire opened up on the entire area at the same time, the first American guns started up somewhat to our right. One of the books [*Four Stars of Hell* by Lawrence Critchell, published by the Declan X. McMullen Publishing Company, 1947] left a bad impression on the conduct of the troopers on the approach to Schijndel. [The book said the troopers were cowering in the ditches, kicked-up by a few officers, and so on.] No doubt everyone was hunting cover, as the fire was murderous. But believe me, most of the men conducted themselves in the true tradition of the trooper.

The Windmill at Eerde
A fine shot of the windmill on the edge of Eerde near the sand dunes, showing a trooper of the 501 below it. Jacob Wingard was killed while observing from an upper window of the windmill. *Krochka*

> I knew the heavy MG fire we were receiving came from a slightly raised position or a small hill. It came in a solid sheet from directly ahead and also down a line to our slight left. As we moved forward, the heaviest fire seemed to be edging slightly

Duel With a Tank
Harry Howard, 1/501, who defied the German tank repeatedly to drape the American flag from the Eerde church steeple and to observe artillery fire. *Homan*

Site of the Duel
A view of the church steeple from which Lt. Harry Howard draped the stars and stripes. German artillery damage is apparent. *US Army*

to our left, which would indicate we were moving at an angle in relation to the fire. The intensity of the fire changed little, which indicated if they moved any MG, they did it fast. I thought I saw a set of tandem tracers, tracers very close together, but not close enough to be coming from the same gun. Naturally, it was impossible to tell about rifle fire at this time. I moved forward at a run for a short distance. Then I saw the railroad tracks and subconsciously knew this was it. The guns had stopped using tracers once they established their zeroing-in.

One of the ammo bearers left 500 rounds of MG ammo in the open field, swept by MG fire. I turned my MG on him and told him he had 10sec to retrieve the ammo. Donald Kane, a squad leader, jumped up, and ran for it, saying, "I'll get it." Sup-

pose he figured the ammo bearer could not muster the nerve, and he would die. Somehow, Kane made it.

Then I heard the Germans, and although they used every device to hide muzzle flashes, I saw a very light spot and moved for it at a dead run.

The double bunker with two MGs was not entered by cowing troopers nor by officers, but by me and close behind me came Carl Tennis.

I suppose someone was decorated for this kicking-up the troops, etc. Perhaps they deserved it, but not at the expense of trying to create the impression that the truly great troopers of the 501 froze-up.

Then we moved almost dead right into Schijndel, which by this time was alive with the noise of battle. I think this was a couple hours before daylight. By daylight, only some sniper fire was going on. I set up on a corner by a building, and sometime later, a noise tapped on the window near me. As I looked, I heard some low muttering and a hand stuck through the window containing some bread. I assumed it was a civilian, too uncertain to make his face visible. I was hungry, but didn't trust the bread to eat it.

A little after daylight, we attacked out of Schijndel, and for a short time as we crossed an open space, it looked like we might be in trouble, but our fire turned the tide, and we broke into their artillery. I am sure you have heard how helpless artillery [units are], once their infantry is stripped, and this turned into a regular turkey shoot. We were using POW's to carry ammo for us as we broke into their artillery. I had one with two bullet holes in the calf of his leg. Finally, Captain Stanley suggested I let him go as a regular POW, as he was going to bleed to death.

Carl Beck of H/501 wrote in his diary of the night attack, saying:

Sept. 22: Field orders came down . . . the battalion is to attack Schijndel. Jumped off about 2300 and everything was quiet until we reached the 155 phase line, then all hell broke loose. We had to dig Krauts out of holes and houses with WP grenades. Kraut wouldn't come out of several places so we blew him out with bazookas. Krauts had a 20mm gun about 1,000 yards away. We went after him with a bazooka and MG but he got away.

Lt. Col. Harry Kinnard
In front of the Eerde church is Lt. Col. Harry Kinnard (West Point, 1939), one of the greatest field commanders to serve the 101st in WWII. Beside him is executive officer, Sammie N. Homan. Homan had commanded F/501 in Normandy and would return to 2/501 as its commander for Bastogne and the duration of the war. *Homan*

During the house to house fighting, Bob Baldwin of G/501 saw Lt. Col. Julian Ewell shoot two Germans in a Dutch living room, using his .45 pistol.

Most resistance in Schijndel ceased before dawn, but a German motorcyclist drove into the village, unaware that the place was now in American hands. He entered an open-air urinal, and a grenade was tossed inside as he was using it. According to Al Luneau of C/501, the mortally wounded German wrote a haunting dying declaration on the porcelain wall using his own blood: "Schwartzes Hand" (Black Hand).

In retrospect, the attack on Schijndel was a short lived but successful foray. The original plan had called for the 3/501 to hold the place until elements of the 502, driving up the highway from St. Oedenrode, could link up. But unexpected pressure on the 502, plus sudden strong attacks against 2/501 from east of Veghel, prompted Colonel Johnson to withdraw his two battalions from Schijndel to consolidate the corridor area once again near Eerde and Veghel.

The attack on Schijndel had netted 250 German POWs, plus 170 wounded and an unknown number killed.

"Fire a Few Rounds at Their Feet!"

Pete Tessoff had joined I/501 as a replacement after Normandy. He received a face wound during the fighting around Eerde. As Pete walked through the village, guarding two German POWs, the trio passed Colonel Johnson, who was standing on the verge of the road.

Seeing the blood from Pete's face wound, the colonel's concern for one of his boys surfaced.

"Did they hurt you son?," the colonel asked. "Fire a few rounds at their feet!"

Later, angered by lack of concern of the British tankers to keep on schedule, Colonel Johnson had words with a tank commander of the British

49

2/501 at the Railroad Crossing
This famous railroad crossing outside Eerde was occupied by numerous 501st troops of assorted companies, as well as by German troops during the see-saw fighting in September. When this photo was taken, 2/501's LMG platoon was holding it. *Krochka*

Generals Taylor (left) and McAuliffe (right) visit Col. Howard R. Johnson (center) at his S-2 office in Eerde. Johnson lost hearing in one ear due to a close exploding shell, and this may have contributed to his death a week later on the island, as he seemingly ignored warnings shouted by a nearby trooper. *Mihok*

Guard's Armored on Hell's Highway. The colonel interrupted the tank commander's tea break, saying, "If you don't get moving, I'll have one of my boy's come out with a screwdriver and a pair of pliers and have him take your tank apart!"

Attack on Eerde

Although the village of Eerde changed hands several times in the early fighting, the most concerted effort failed against G/501 on 24 September.

Tex McMorries was recommended for the Distinguished Service Cross (DSC) for his actions in repulsing the attack on 24 September. Using his A-4 MG, he was credited with 38 kills that day. Tex was responsible also for knocking out two MG42's and a 20mm cannon and crew.

Tex wrote about certain details of the event:

Our position served as a roadblock and the point of an inverted-V defense line. Our lines ran along the road for a ways, then left the road and swung back towards the windmill. My position was farthest north, or northwest on the road. On 23–24

Visiting His Flock
Father Francis Sampson, the 501's Catholic chaplain, visiting members of his flock on a motorcycle in September 1944.

September, they estimate the Germans dropped over 600 mortar rounds near our gun. We had heard a tank, and having no mines, we dug out in front before the attack, simulating burying mines. They had a tank with this attack; it came in very close, gun down, firing at us, supporting their infantry. The tank stopped almost as if it had spotted mines. This attack came four times, the first three determined, the last disheartened.

We ran very low on ammunition in my position, which I believe was receiving the brunt. Captain Kraeger or someone sent word, and they were stripping rifle ammo and reloading it in belts for me.

The Germans made a bad mistake—they should have attacked farther north or farther south, then they wouldn't have exposed their troops to our perfect field of fire. Perhaps in the beginning, they picked this because of their use of tanks, but when they failed to go all out in gambling the loss of their

tanks, they ended up with a very bad place to attack. Also, they perhaps had too much confidence in their artillery preparation for the attack. It failed to eliminate many gun positions. It appeared every few yards was hit by a shell, but only direct hits or real close shells were effective.

You see, nobody had a better view than I did. In fact, later, a few other people made their way up to my position to get a better report and view of the scene and the spoils of the battle. The killing grounds lay on the road, in and near the ditches, from 50 to 200yd north or northwest of our position. We counted over 100 weapons laying on the ground in front of us, from 20mm to pistols, from 25yd out to almost 200yd.

Tex's objective narrative omits much of the drama of this battle, but bear in mind that the enemy began the attack with numeric superiority and tank support, being halted only by infantry small arms fire and tactical superiority. The outcome was definitely in question, but this was to become a

Peter Frank and a German Paratrooper
Sergeant Peter Frank served on IPW Team Number 9 with the 501. A native of Belgium, he spoke Basque French, as well as German. Note the tough-looking Fallschirmjager POW leaning against the wall at left, wearing a boat-shaped overseas cap. The pocket for his gravity-blade jump knife is visible on his right leg. *Musura*

common scenario in the 101st Airborne's late-war battles.

Twice during Market-Garden, McMorries was cited for the DSC, but his platoon and squad sergeants, Haun and Case, stated they wanted to re-write the citations before submitting them. When Bastogne came up unexpectedly, Haun was killed and Case was blinded, and the write-ups were never sent through channels.

The outcome of other attacks on Eerde were no less uncertain until the battles had been won, and the coming narratives concerning Carl Beck and friends on a different flank are a good example.

Prior to Market-Garden, two officers of the 501, who had served with service company in Normandy, were transferred into 3/501 as rifle platoon leaders. They were Lt. Francis Sheridan and Lt. Charles K. Davidson. Both officers proved to be outstanding in combat, but Lieutenant Davidson didn't last long.

Carl Beck's combat diary again sheds light on further German attempts to take Eerde from the west flank:

Sept. 25: Made contact with the Herman Goring Division . . . they were on a combat patrol . . . sure went around and round til after dark. Duffy got a slug in the pack, and I got my beanie turned around on my head by a bunch of MG fire. Darn close. Finally got knocked back into the ditch when a sniper's bullet hit a tree right beside my head. Knocked me coo-coo for awhile and a few splinters in my face, but nothing serious. Two wounded Krauts in our ditch . . . finally pulled back with one prisoner and left all wounded. No casualties, but

Lieutenant Davidson got slugs through his pack and patch pockets and canteen. He sure is in solid with the platoon now. I didn't think anyone could move, but he sure did. We are sure proud of him.

Sept. 26: Moved up to take over part of the line between I company and 2nd Battalion. Ran right smack into an element of German paratroopers. Met them halfway and sure got a mess of them. A corporal in the 1st Platoon is dead and another private, besides. Lieutenant Davidson, Aubin, Duffy, and I were out abreast of the 3rd Platoon and Lieutenant Davidson was killed by an LMG in the chest. Aubin got his .45 . . . took us about two hours to drive them off and there is dead Krauts laying all around—sure was hot for awhile. Must have got about 35 Krauts. Johnson was killed by a machine pistol, but Schleibaum got that Kraut. Pulled back about a hundred yards and set up final protective line . . . dead Kraut laying here and we had to cover him with sugar beets. Got Kraut parachute wings and a wallet with Kraut FPL in it. Turned it in to S-2. Quiet nite after we got dug in.

Sept. 27: Krauts hit us with one company and an LMG platoon in support. Fired about 2,000 rounds, and then it started to rain. Stayed in a squatting position for about 3-1/2 hours. Bones was shot between the eyes and Wilks tried to fix his eyes. About half the 1st Platoon was wiped out by the first 12-round barrage. Ground looks plowed over and the bark is torn off all the trees. Got a new platoon leader today but didn't see him during the whole battle . . . a few Krauts out this morning and Laf Otis reported no activity after taking out a patrol. Carried Bones out and Turner got his pistol. Poor guy. One of the spark plugs of this platoon.

The Lost Division

Company H had sustained so many losses in repulsing the Germans that D Company was sent over from 2/501 to reinforce their line. Sergeant Jurecko wrote in his diary:

Sept. 28: A beautiful day today, but last night, it rained very hard and with the rain came death to eight of our men. We pulled in here (my platoon) last night to help out H company who were taking a terrific beating. Along this road lined with high trees, enemy shells hit the trees and threw shrapnel right into the men's foxholes and killed or wounded quite a few. It's a helluva bloody mess along this road—bodies lying everywhere, both of the enemy and our boys. Its been eleven days since we jumped here. How I would like to take off my boots and wash my feet or even shave my face. The men are very tired and worn out. They need rest bad.

Airborne Artillerymen
A 75mm pack howitzer crew from A/377 man their gun in
Holland. Left to right: Charles Eckert, Frank Waas, and Orland "Pappy" Fry. *via Benecke*

Other Jurecko diary entries from Holland:

I got a hold of a *Stars & Stripes* and they have us in print as the "Lost Division." Well it seems that we are lost. Very little food, sleep, or rest; the men have been fighting hard and being wounded or killed. Yet they keep fighting and will not stop until the British Infantry reach us.

Also:

Yes, I saw men of steel with tears in their eyes. The day Sgt. Choate, my first sergeant was shot through the head, and I told Sergeant Koss of it, his best friend . . . there, amidst the hell and furious noise along the front lines of battle I saw tears come to the eyes of the bearded young sergeant and watched him break to pieces at the loss of his comrade.

After the Battle
After the 101st left the Eerde area, Canadian engineers reportedly plowed the sand dunes flat to convert the wide open area to a temporary airstrip.

Today, the windmill at the north edge of town still stands, although the top portion, including the wind blades is missing. A small but attractive monument to the 501, with a stone mosaic of the Geronimo insignia, stands right in front of the windmill.

Chapter Seven

Veghel and Uden

The city of Veghel was at the top of the 101st's initial bridgehead. Two bridges were seized there—over the Willems-Vaart Canal at the south edge of town and the Aa River, in town. Members of the 501's S-2 section ran into Veghel from the DZ near Eerde, and Chief Sayers and friends were the first to arrive. They shot up a German cyclist and captured a few members of the local German garrison. Chief then entered a house to celebrate. He discovered a bottle of orange liquid, exclaimed, "Apricot brandy!" and gulped the contents. It turned out to be orange dye, which left Sayers' lips, tongue, and teeth a strange color for the next two weeks.

Dutch residents started filling the streets and celebrating their liberation in what Lt. Bill Sefton calls "a comic opera war." Priests handed out beer and pretzels, girls danced with the soldiers in the streets, and Dutch resistance men flocked in with information on German troop movements.

There was brief excitement as a group of Germans tried to escape from town in a bus. The vehicle was riddled with bullets and crashed. One of the passengers was a 14-year-old Hitler Youth in full Nazi uniform. Sefton recalled, "He was so snottily defiant that I think the majority of our group shared my great desire to turn him over my knee and paddle his ass with the butt of a weapon."

Sefton also saw a German tank struck by a perfectly aimed bazooka round as it approached Veghel from the south. The round hit the tank's turret, then went up in the air because they had forgotten to pull the pin in the nose of the rocket. The Nazi tank drove into the square, then fled from town with no casualties to either side. Being the farthest north of 101st units, the job of the 501 at Veghel was to defend the town against German counterattacks, holding open this section of the corridor.

Hand-to-Hand

Unknown to the Americans who had occupied Veghel so easily on 17 September, a battalion-size German force was encroaching on the town from the direction of S'Hertogensbosch, along the canal. This powerful thrust would fall squarely on the perimeter of E/501 in the wee hours of the morning. A small German probe came into the A/501 sector to the north near the Aa River.

Frank H. Whiting, an A/501 replacement, was spending his first night in combat. Frank had spent most of the 17th doing a lot of marching, without encountering the enemy. At 0200 of the 18th, he was about to have a hairy baptism of fire. Placed in an outpost in a swampy area near the railroad embankment, the exhausted trooper soon dozed off. He awakened when several German pointmen crawled into his hole. They grunted in German and informed him with prods of their weapons that he was their prisoner. Leaving one man behind to guard Whiting, the German scouts continued on quietly to the east. Whiting was still awakening and comprehending his predicament, when he heard the voice of Sgt. Bruce Fess from Chicago, call out to see if he was OK. The German guarding Whiting panicked and fired a rifle shot toward Fess. Whiting grabbed the Mauser rifle, trying to wrest it away.

The Well-Dressed Paratrooper

Sergeant Adam Slusher of C/326 demonstrates what the well-dressed paratrooper was wearing in late 1944. On his head is the knit wool cap, commonly worn under the helmet. He wears an O.D. wool shirt under his sleeveless knit-wool sweater. The 101st Div. shoulder patch is visible on his left shoulder. He wears the Air Corps-type suspenders with leather end loops to secure his M-43 combat trousers along with a captured German belt. The trousers have been modified into jump pants by adding a canvass cargo pocket to each leg, as well as tie-down straps. An M-3 trench knife at the ankle and jump boots (contrary to prevailing rules) complete his accouterments. A Thompson sub-machine gun is his weapon of choice. *Slusher*

Both men rose from the hole, grappling for possession of the weapon. Fumbling and pawing, they dropped the weapon and rolled into the swamp. Whiting's comrades behind the embankment could

After the withdrawal of the mixed battalion that attacked E/501 from S'Hertogensbosch, some German survivors were rounded up as prisoners on 18 September 1944. A barrage of 60mm mortar fire had dazed and demoralized many of them. *Krochka*

hear the commotion, but in the darkness, could only guess at what was going on.

With frenzied thrashing in the muddy water, neither opponent could attain a good grip on the other. They bit flesh and gouged at each other's eyes. Whiting choked the German almost unconscious, but received a bite in return, his finger being chewed almost to the bone.

Thinking that Whiting had been killed, Fess and Morris Bull Bear tossed grenades over the embankment. During his struggle, Whiting could feel and hear the explosions on either side of him. Then, he remembered the rifle. Exhausted, he broke free of the German and crawled, groping for it in the blackness. He located the rifle and swung it like a ball bat, striking the German in the head repeatedly. Whiting was exhausted but victorious. Hands greasy with mud, he staggered to his feet, worked the rifle bolt and aimed at the German, who had raised up to all fours from the ground. Whiting fired a round into the German's back, putting him flat on the ground.

Lieutenant Mosier ran up and asked, "Are you OK?"

Whiting could only point at the prone figure and let the rifle drop.

Mosier quickly withdrew his M-3 knife and dropped on the German, stabbing him several times.

Frank Whiting would go on to fight through Market-Garden, and the Battle of Bastogne, but this was his first and last hand-to-hand fight. Members of E/501 were about to experience pointblank fighting near the canal.

Night Attack

Captured Machine Guns
Some of the machine guns captured from the German bat-talion that struck at E/501 the first night in Holland are displayed by their captors. *US Army*

The German group that marched along the canal the night of 17–18 September was a mixed battalion minus one company, with some paratroops attached. Their route of travel brought them directly to the outpost line (OPLR) of E/501's 2nd Platoon. Behind this at the railroad embankment was the front line. Behind the front line was a large building housing a phosphate factory.

When E/501 scouts reported hearing voices and footsteps to their front, S/Sgt. Frank McClure went to investigate. He later recalled:

> I went down the road about 100yd with "Guadalcanal Clark," past Garcia and Moore, who were dug in beside the road. I heard voices and Garcia said, "Halt! Who goes there?" That was the start of the fight. Garcia jumped into the canal because a grenade went off right on the edge of his foxhole. When I saw him later, it had blacked his eye and the whole side of his face. He swam to safety on the other side. The Germans had them little stinkin' grenades on the end of their rifles, similar to ours, but they looked like a little CO_2 bottle sittin' there. Those things would come in, and they'd really jolt you. Clark and I dived over the roadway, started running, and ran into a fence. The fence knocked us down, which probably saved our lives. Well, the momentum of these people was terrific. They just kept coming, they came on, they spread out . . . The attack eventually flowed north. It couldn't go south because of the canal and couldn't go forward because of Lightfoot's machine gun. Clark and I went through the pasture, came back through Joyner's squad, then back through the fac-

A member of E/501 inspects some German POWs. *Krochka*

tory, and back around in behind Lightfoot. By that time, *everybody* was involved in the fight. There was some hand-to-hand stuff that went on because they had actually rolled right up on Joyner's people.

Harry Mole, the E/501 wire corporal, was with Lt. Joseph MacGregor when the shooting began. MacGregor ordered Harry to stay in position with Russell Waller, to maintain a 2nd Platoon CP, then vanished into the dark to join the fight. Soon thereafter, Waller became worried about his friend, Walter Olender, known as "Geezel."

"I've got to find him, he's never been in combat without me," Waller said.

"But MacGregor said to stay here til he comes back . . ."

Waller ran off toward the right to look for Geezel. He was caught in the fight and never returned. In the light of morning, he was found dead, lying next to his buddy Geezel.

Company E eventually faded back behind the railroad embankment, and Harry Mole found himself alone on the enemy side at dawn. He realized he

Rounding Up POWs
A 501st trooper rounding up Germans in Veghel. *Krochka*

was maintaining a platoon CP without a platoon. He later recalled "hightailing it back to the tracks, and I think I jumped over the embankment in one

Tactical Conference in Veghel
Colonel Bud Harper, CO of the 327, with Maj. Gen. Maxwell Taylor. *Krochka*

Resistance Fighters Meet Glider Medics
Combat medics from the 327 pose with Dutch resistance fighters near the corner facing the Veghel church. *Dutch photo via Hopke*

bound, as there was a German after me. He wasn't firing. I think he was out to get a prisoner so they could find out who was in Veghel that day."

Survivors of the German battalion continued firing until 1100 that morning, and E/501 moved forward to reclaim their old line. Forty dazed prisoners were rounded up. Most of the German dead and wounded had been dragged back when the battalion withdrew. Frank McClure recalled:

I remember seeing one German laying behind a pretty good sized tree. Somebody had shot right through it and still hit him. We heard there were still some of our guys out there, mainly MacGregor and them . . . Abshire was captured. Bobbitt Waller, Wright, "Oakie" Morris, and Olender were killed. Ramirez was my man, and I found him in the ditch, in some kind of a coma. They just had beat the hell out of him. Hadn't shot him, but they beat him up real bad. Our guys were lying in a ditch and some of them didn't have a mark on them. One of the guys was shot up pretty good. We had seen guys shot or tore up with mortar shells or artillery, but I didn't recall seeing anybody dead without any marks on them. Of course everybody was real jit-

tery after that. It was a scary thing; I remember that spooked everybody real bad for a long time. We kept moving out and thinking we were going to get into another big fight, but the 1st Platoon started rounding up prisoners, and whatever happened, there was no more fight left in them guys.

Lieutenant MacGregor had been shot through his helmet and sustained a horrible head wound. He was barely alive when recaptured, and the Germans left him for dead. As medics carried Mac from the battlefield, his men examined the bloody, bullet-holed helmet, and doubted that even Mac could survive such a wound.

A large, dynamic leader of men, MacGregor was a Scottish citizen who had lived in the Bronx before the war. He had been an outstanding soccer player and had won the title "Mr. New York City" for his weightlifting accomplishments. Miraculously, he would be back for more fighting.

E/501's action was the first of many desperate battles to hold Veghel against German attacks.

Sergeant Leo Gillis of F/501 had been put in charge of an outpost on the east edge of town. On the second day, he saw a tremendous German artillery barrage work across Veghel, and "it looked like they were going to blow the town right off the map."

Gillis rounded-up his troops, and they headed west to link-up with friendly forces. He recalled:

We had seen hundreds of Dutch civilians, all wearing orange, heading into Veghel. We tried to talk to them, but they smiled and kept walking; they were going to have a big celebration. When them people were all in that town, the Germans started to shell it, and it was just fantastic. That town caught fire, and there was smoke and shells, and it just seemed like they were going to blow the town right up-completely. It really got bad. We stopped a couple of times because I didn't want to get in too close to that artillery. I remember down in these sewers and pipes, women and children were down there, and they were crying. That artillery had a habit of making people cry—especially women.

Cummings Wins a Silver Star

By 21 September, the 327 had been moved north from the Zonsche Forest to join the fight at Veghel. On that day, T/Sgt. Ernest Cummings of C/327 won the first of two Silver Stars he would collect in WWII.

Losing one man of his squad killed in an ambush, Cummings sent the others to the left while he circled to the right. Advancing to within 15yd of an enemy MG nest, he destroyed it with grenades and Tommygun fire. He then led his squad in an attack, killing 20 Germans and capturing 30 more. At dawn on the 22nd, Cummings and his squad repulsed a German counterattack. Cummings crawled out under fire to rescue a wounded comrade.

Elements of the 506 moved up from Son to assist in the Veghel fighting, with 3/506 doing much infantry fighting. Other elements moved beyond to Uden to the north, and some were surrounded there briefly, under command of Col. Charles Chase. The 1/506 was sent south to Koevering on the 24th to reopen the highway when the British convoy there was wiped out.

Hitching to Nijmegen

During this period, a number of regimental S-2 men of the 501 hitched a ride north with the British convoy to Nijmegen (in the 82nd Airborne's sector), which was still occupied by the Germans. The group established themselves in a hotel, and were discovered. They then shot their way out. In the escape, King R. Palmer was killed.

Heavy German attacks crashed against Veghel on 22–24 September with 3/506 and elements of the 326 and the 327 holding the south and west approaches. During one attack, Pfc. Anthony Yodis of H/506 crossed the canal and went forward eagerly

The German Paratrooper's Creed
Exerpts from the German Paratrooper's Creed follow:
You are the chosen ones of the German Army. You will seek combat and train yourself to endure any manner of test. To you the battle shall be the fulfillment.

Cultivate true comradeship, for by the aid of your comrades you will conquer or die. Beware of talking. Be not corruptible. Men act while women chatter. Chatter may bring you to the grave. Be calm and prudent, strong and resolute. Valour and the enthusiasm of an offensive spirit will cause you to prevail in the attack.

The most precious thing in the presence of the foe is ammunition. He who shoots uselessly, merely to comfort himself is a man of straw. He is a weakling who merits not the title of paratrooper.

Never surrender. To you death or victory must be a point of honor.

You can triumph only if your weapons are good. See to it that you submit yourself to this law—first my weapons and then myself.

You must grasp the full purport of every enterprise, so that if your leader be killed you can yourself fulfill it.

Against an open foe, fight with chivalry, but to a guerrilla, extend no quarter.

Keep your eyes wide open. Tune yourself to the topmost pitch. Be as nimble as a greyhound, as tough as leather, as hard as Krupp steel, and so you shall be the German Warrior incarnate.

Troopers of C/326
Members of C/326 paused for a photo between Veghel and Uden, Holland. Top row, left to right: Onsbey, Gaston, Minar, Adam Slusher, and Hanko. Below, left to right: Lawson, Cawley, Albert Kouba, and McCarthy. *Slusher*

to meet the advancing Germans. He was killed in that action.

The 501 met most of the attacks from Erp to the southeast and generally held the east sector. Jack Rider, a 2/501 cook, knocked out a German tank with a bazooka. Clerk Joe Mero engaged the enemy near a grain elevator and killed many. His binoculars were shot away during the fight. A day or two later, he was fatally wounded.

The Veghel fighting proved that infantrymen with small arms and bazookas could sometimes prevail against tanks, as a matter of necessity. This lesson would prove invaluable in later fighting at Bastogne.

Kinnard's Cannae

On 20 September, Lt. Col. Harry Kinnard (CO of 1/501) maneuvered the entire battalion on an aggressive sweep toward Dinter and Heeswijk, to disrupt and rout enemy troops massing there to counterattack Veghel. Using HQ/1, A/501, and B/501 to advance north of and parallel to the Williams-Vaart Canal, Kinnard also positioned elements of C/501 in a backstop area to intercept the German retreat. A total encirclement, or cannae, was accomplished, with 418 prisoners taken; another 40 Germans were killed. The herd of German POWs was paraded through Veghel later that day, down streets lined with jeering Dutch civilians.

"Holy Christ! He's Gonna Take Over This Joint!"

On patrol outside Veghel one afternoon, several men from F/501, including Leo Gillis, encountered a hard-core German non-com who wished to negotiate a truce to pick up wounded. This German sergeant didn't think he should have to surrender his pistol. Jim Nadeau was also in the group that captured him. The German was taken into HQ/2 501. Bill Russo recalled:

I was at battalion HQ; they had taken the man's gun. They had not blindfolded him. This guy was infuriated, because if you're not blindfolded, you can't go back. You should have heard him—believe me. I thought, *Holy Christ! He's gonna take over this joint!* He had the Iron Cross, buddy, and you could see that he had earned it. He *looked* soldier, he *acted*

60

Parachute Tent
A dugout covered with green camouflaged parachute nylon, providing some concealment from German aerial observation. *Krochka*

soldier, everything he did was soldier! I thought: *My God! Thank God they don't have too many of them floating around*!

He said, "My men will think I deserted them! Do you realize what you're doing?" You know, like: You dumb sonsabitches. He was somethin'. I think anybody who met him—they met a soldier!

"I Don't Think We Should Do That, Soldier"
One afternoon in Veghel, General Taylor saw Eugene "Red" Flanagan marching a German prisoner purposefully toward the Willems-Vaart Canal. Sensing something was amiss, Taylor noticed that the German's hands were bound behind his back.

"Where are you going with that prisoner, trooper?" Flanagan pointed to the brown American jump boots on the POWs feet. "Gonna drown this bastard in the canal, general."

"I don't think we should do that, soldier," said Taylor, as he gently removed the POW from Flanagan's custody.

More Defensive Action

In one defensive action by 2/501, Charlie Eckman and Gleason Roberts set up their gun in support of a squad led by Asher Hetrick from E/501. Eckman recalled:

We set up our gun near a shoe factory on the edge of Veghel and got into some hellish fighting there. Asher Hetrick of E/501 was to my right; he had seven guys with him. He said, "Don't worry about the fourteen Krauts that's coming up the lane; we'll get them with the first volley." I never even gave those Germans a thought, because I knew they'd get them. Gleason and I opened up. He used the machine gun, and I used the Thompson sub. My God, they were just comin' in waves. They even shot ack-ack at us, and they knocked out our machine gun. That's where I got some more shrapnel in my leg, but it wasn't bad, just bleeding and stuff. Those cannon shells explode, and that damn stuff cuts all through the trees. When they take it out of you, it *grinds*. Going in is no problem. Two of Hetrick's guys got killed . . . But by Jesus, we just kept firing and for some reason, they didn't overrun us and kill us. We didn't have anything left to fight with. Hetrick's men had killed all the Germans on the lane,

Taking Ten
Albert A. Krochka, then one of the 101st's divisional photographers, takes ten on a Dutch street. He has replaced his torn jumpsuit with the M43 model and is armed with an M-3 grease gun. *Krochka*

and it looked to me like on the field that Gleason and I had killed twenty-some before they stopped coming. Hell, they had tanks and ack-ack, and they could have overrun us.

Eckman's account is somewhat typical of the many desperate battles to hold Veghel. The soft sandy soil in the area enabled men to dig deep holes with ease, and many tunneled in sideways as well. Artillery experienced from the inside of such a hole was doubly terrifying, as the whole earth seemed to shift and move.

Lieutenant Werner Meier, the interrogator, pris-

oners of war (IPW) officer for the 501 kept a list of the name, rank, and branch of every prisoner taken in the Veghel-Eerde area for the first two days. The first day's bag included 25 Germans of whom there was a paymaster, one lieutenant, three SS troopers, one Hitler Youth, and two Dutch civilians. On the second day, the list had more than doubled to 55 POWs. After that, the list was so long, that Meier didn't bother to list all the POWs individually.

Reopening the Highway

When the Germans wiped out a long convoy of British vehicles south of Veghel, near Koevering on

C-47 Crash
Sergeant Benecke paused on the trip to the Island to photograph this crash-landed C-47 of the 79th TCS, 439th TCG. It is probable that this plane was delivering gliders bearing the 325th GIR (82nd Airborne) to the Overasselt LZ when the flight was aborted short of the LZ. Note the glider in rear. The *Cherokee Strip* nose art title is visible on the plane. *Benecke*

24 September, an estimated 300 British soldiers were killed by 40mm antiaircraft guns and swarming infantry. Afterward, 1/506 came down from Uden to reopen the highway. Spending the night in fields west of the highway were A/ and C/506. It rained during the night, and a small group of German paratroopers got lost and wandered into an American position. Someone fired on them with a Tommy-gun, and the survivors bolted over a hedgerow, dropping right into the laps of a C/506 group under Lt. Albert Hassenzahl.

One of Hassenzahl's men, Robert Wiatt, was standing in a ditch below the hedge when he heard the shots and then realized that men were hurtling over the hedge into the ditch with him. In the extreme darkness, he kept quiet because he couldn't tell if the intruders were friend or foe. One of the new arrivals lay on the bottom of the ditch with his arms wrapped around Wiatt's feet. Suddenly a voice spoke in German, and a wild melee erupted in the ditch.

Lieutenant Hassenzahl found himself fighting with a pot-bellied German. He punched the man in the midsection, heard him deflate like a balloon, then grabbed his trench knife and plunged it into the German, although the wound wasn't fatal.

Wiatt kept trying to kick his legs loose from the arms of the prone German. Wiatt grabbed his M-1 rifle, to which he had previously affixed a bayonet, and plunged it downward into the German. The next day he discovered that the blade had taken the man through the throat. Several Germans survived the confused brawl to be taken prisoner. Wiatt and others looped parachute suspension line around the neck of each prisoner, linking them together in one line.

A few troopers began marching them to an area along the highway. This movement in darkness was difficult and while climbing over a fence, one of the Germans tripped and fell, dragging the others down too. Thinking that the American paratroopers had killed one of their number in cold blood, the others began letting out with terrified screams. Somehow, the prisoners were handed over to a headquarters unit for safekeeping.

The next day, both A/ and C/506 encountered some Lend-Lease Sherman tanks that had been captured from the British and were now being used by the Germans. Leonard Benson of A/506 noticed a black cross painted on a Sherman that was driving alongside his platoon. He mounted the tank, banged on the turret and captured an entire Nazi crew.

Sergeant Bill Knight of C/506 saw another Sherman drive out of the woods with crying Dutch civilians on the outside. The tank fired at the Americans, then backed out of sight into the woods again. The Germans had evidently coerced these women and children to perform the role of shields against retaliatory gunfire.

Knight saw another enemy Sherman flipped over by an exploding Gammon grenade. He and Cpl. George Rollyson caught a large group of German infantry by surprise in a long ditch. The pair of Americans shot dozens of Germans there in less than a minute but were never recognized for the feat.

After a total of 44hr, the highway near Koevering was open once again.

Elements of the division began moving north, beyond Uden and Grave in the 82nd Airborne's sector and then on to Nijemegen. Crossing onto the island of land between the Waal and Neder Rhine Rivers, the 506 and their supporting artillery—the 321—led the way. After staging near the Zetten-Andelst railroad station, they moved west on the Island to occupy an insignificant Dutch town already held by the British Army. The town was called Opheusden.

The 501, led by 1st Bn. would cross the Nijmegen Bridge, then head east to Coffin Corner east of Driel, to take up positions along the Neder Rhine.

A whole new phase of the 101st's history was beginning-the saga of the muddy, bloody piece of land that became known as the Island.

Chapter Eight

Coffin Corner

A 30ft-high dirt embankment with a road running along the top extends from the south shore of the Neder Rhine just below Arnhem, westward past Driel, Heteren Rankwijk, and Opheusden. Although this dike, which runs parallel to the south shore of the Neder Rhine, is there to withhold any drastic flooding of the river, it is, at places, several hundred yards from the water's edge. The dike and road run fairly straight while the river zig-zags such that at some spots the river is fairly close to the dike and at other spots is a considerable distance away.

Traveling west along the dike road from just below Arnhem, the situation is much the same geographically, as one passes under the railroad bridge that crosses the dike at right angles, after crossing the Neder Rhine, between Arnhem and Driel, then continuing past Heteren and beyond.

The spot where the then destroyed railroad bridge passes over the dike road became known to 1944 paratroopers as "Coffin Corner." The area north of (on the water side of) the dike was held by German troops, with their backs to the Neder Rhine. The area east of the railroad bridge was also held by German troops, and continued to be during October and November. Thus, US troops in the area were faced with Germans to their front and all along their left flank-the railroad embankment being part of the German front-line.

When 1/501 moved up in an orchard near Coffin Corner in the darkness of 4 October 1944, the corner was relinquished by Commonwealth troops, who had held the area very tentatively against local German efforts.

The Germans in the area belonged to the 60th Armored Inf. (panzer-grenadier) Reg. of the 116th Div.

James Calvin, an enlisted replacement in C/501 for the Holland invasion, described the early fighting at Coffin Corner:

We marched about 6hr in the dead of night to relieve the British just below Arnhem, between the two rivers in what we called the Island. In October, we had a defense line set up about 40yd behind and parallel to a dike. As I remember it, we called it the Coffin Corner. They stopped our advance a few hundred yards from the position we were supposed to occupy. They called the officers forward to reconnoiter the position. We had fallen out to the side, and I had my back against an apple tree. I remember at the time seeing Capt. Robert Phillips, who equaled and even surpassed the essence of all great leaders, coming up through the orchard, walking as though he was not afraid to be killed. He shouted out orders to the platoon leaders, telling them what he wanted them to do. In looking back, I am certain that the Germans thought he was directing the actions of the battalion and not of the company. It was for this reason that I believe now, and have through the years, that they pulled back-thinking a battalion was on the attack.

We relieved the British within 30–40min, and we occupied this position for the next three or four days.

Aerial View of Coffin Corner
Coffin Corner is visible where the railroad bridge crosses the road on the south edge of the river. The curve near the upper right of the photo is where the Germans detonated an aerial bomb to blow open the dike and flood the area as far west as Opheusden. *Coby De Haartog*

The next morning, just about daybreak, a sniper in a farmhouse to our right rear zeroed-in on one of our people, S/Sgt. William R. Roark. I will never forget this. Roark was a fine individual. I heard the shot, and I heard that awful sound that told me it hit some kind of target; we called for Roark, and he didn't answer. I took my rifle off my shoulder; he was three or four foxholes from me. I crawled down the line to his position, and he had slumped down into his foxhole. When he did, his helmet slid over the front of his face. I reached down and pulled the helmet back, and I saw immediately that Roark didn't know what hit him. He was dead. I returned to my position.

Within 30–40min, Captain Phillips called for this man, Sgt. Milton F. Nelson, from Minnesota. I'll say at the outset that Nelson was no doubt the greatest, the bravest combat soldier I ever knew. He reported to the CP on a dead run. Within 5–10min he returned and announced he needed to take two people on a recon patrol. I didn't say anything, but I knew I would be selected. I don't think there was a GI anywhere who went on more patrols than I did, and I have to admit, I ran scared every step of the way.

Nelson selected Casada, and by then I already had my combat equipment on, because I knew he was going to holler for me.

Captain Phillips wanted Nelson to return to the orchard, which was visible, and draw their fire, so that he could ascertain the probable enemy strength in this farmhouse.

Our mission was simply to parallel to the right to a hedgerow, then proceed to the front of the orchard, then return back up the exact route we took the night before. When we came to the front of the orchard, I was in the center, Sergeant Nelson was on my left, and Casada was on my right . . . They opened up on us with machine guns, and I don't honestly know how we got out of that orchard alive. We returned to our lines in the same way that we came in. Casada dropped off at his platoon, and I continued on with Sergeant Nelson. We were no more than 30–40yd from our CP when I heard the shot. Nelson was running to the right and a few steps in front of me. I heard this awful sound, and I knew that the bullet had found its target. Nelson was shot through his left arm, through his chest, and out his right side. He fell like a ton of bricks. They sent people out from the CP to help me bring him in. When we brought Nelson in, he was cussing like a sailor. This was the bravest man I ever knew. But before he died—and I'm sure his lungs were filled up with blood—he did not cry out loud, but I saw tears from his eyes. Bless his heart; he was the greatest individual I ever knew.

Two or three weeks later, Captain Bob received a letter from his mother after she had learned of his death. In the first paragraph she designated that she wanted this letter to go to whomever was with her son when he was killed. They gave me the letter and I carried it. When I was wounded at Bastogne, it was severely enough that they cut my clothes off and I lost her letter, her address, and all my notes. But I would dearly love to meet with this lady and tell her what a great, great individual, and what a courageous son she really had. I don't remember her first name, I remember only Nelson.

When Nelson was killed, they made Crews the squad leader and made me assistant squad leader. This was no more than a corporal's stripes. I had been in the Army over four years and had already reached the grade of staff sergeant before I transferred into the paratroopers. But with all of the promotions I had up until that time, this promotion meant the most to me, simply because I gained it in combat.

With the frequent shifting of companies and regiments along the dike, 1/501 was eventually replaced at Coffin Corner by D/506. Frank Anness recalled moving into the area, along with an airborne artillery battalion.

A pesky German with an MP40 machine pistol was dug-in on the railroad embankment on the right flank. Each evening at exactly 1800hr, he would raise up in his hole and spray a full magazine of 9mm into the American positions, then duck back out of sight.

Anness consulted with an artilleryman about this situation and together, they bore-sighted a 105mm howitzer on the precise spot where the German popped-up each evening. When the German made his next appearance, he disappeared in a burst of flame and debris as the 105 took him out.

The only serious attack against US positions at the corner was made by a Mk IV Sturmgeschutz and some grenadiers one evening while C/501 held the area. Frank Carpenter of that unit bore-sighted an abandoned British 6-pounder cannon at the Mk IV when it rumbled through the underpass below the railroad bridge and turned south, exposing itself broadside to American fire. Frank chambered a round in the cannon and didn't know how to fire it. He began striking every lever in sight until the weapon discharged. The round streaked directly into the Mk IV, knocking it out. Expert riflemen of the 501 picked off the grenadiers. Frank Carpenter was later decorated with the Silver Star for this action.

Chapter Nine

Dike Warfare—Opheusden, Randwijk, and Heteren

After reaching the area known as the Island, 3/506 moved from the Zetten-Andelst area, westward to the town of Opheusden. The 2/506 occupied the dike facing the Neder (Lower) Rhine river on a line extending eastward toward Randwijk. The line west of Opheusden ran south, crossing the east–west railroad line at right angles. Company H held this line on either side of the track, with G/506 extending from their right flank into the town and around to the east along the dike.

First Platoon of H/506 was along the road that crosses the track, which then goes north into

Silver Star
General Matt Ridgeway, XVIII Airborne Corps commander, looks on as Gen. Lewis Brereton awards the Silver Star to Sgt. Ralph Bennett. Bennett served as a squad leader with H/506 at Opheusden.*US Army*

Opheusden from the southwest. Moving into the area was easy, and the British troops who pulled out at that time remarked that it had been a quiet sector. It was 4 October 1944, and the Germans would begin a furious drive to capture Opheusden the next morning.

Attack on 5 October

Hank DiCarlo, Joe Harris, and other H/501 men were near a blockhouse made of railroad ties, west of the road and just south of the track. At dawn on the 5th, they were aware of Germans moving to their front. Small-arms fire came along the track from the west any time someone moved next to the blockhouse.

Major Oliver Horton, CO of 3/506, came up that morning to look the situation over. He peeked around the corner of the blockhouse, and Harris yelled not to walk out by the track, as the area was under fire. Horton ignored the warning, walked out near the railroad track, and was hit by enemy fire. A medic gave him aid, but he died within an hour. Major Robert Harwick was 3/506 CO once again.

Over on the right flank, north of the railroad track, H's 2nd and 3rd Platoons were experiencing devastating mortar and artillery fire (the British said it was the worst barrage since El Alamein), followed by wave upon wave of infantry. Sergeant Charles Richard's squad was overrun by weight of numbers, and the survivors circled around to rejoin the company. Lieutenant Alex Andros and his men piled up scores of German bodies in front of their positions.

Some German troops made their way into town

Battlefield Commission
Fred Bahlau served with HQ/3 506 in Holland and won a second Silver Star at Opheusden. The ribbon with cluster is visible in this photo. Not long thereafter, Fred received a battlefield commission and was transferred into C/506 as a lieutenant for the duration of the war. *Bahlau*

Ambush Site
A group of 101st troops in front of the Opheusden railroad station, where 1st Sgt. Fred Bahlau, Ben Hiner, and Lieutenant Weisenberger ambushed a company of Germans. *Krochka*

for house-to-house fighting. Ed Slizewski of G/506 was in a building in town when his buddy John Androsky staggered-in the door and said, "Polack Eddie, I've got a gut full of lead." He then dropped dead to the floor.

Joe Harris saw a badly wounded runner of G/506 in the battalion aid station. The wounded man told Harris to go to the house used as G/506's CP to look for a musette bag behind the boiler in the cellar. Someone had blown the safe in the brick factory across from Wageningen and had placed the paper guilders in this bag, hiding the loot in the cellar of the CP. Upon checking the location out, it was discovered that someone had tossed a white-phosphorus (WP) grenade into the cellar, and the bag of money had burned up.

The 1/506 was moved forward to support 3/506 in holding Opheusden. Lieutenant Bill Pyne was CO of C/506. He went up onto the main dike to have a look toward the river and was struck by an exploding shell, sustaining a serious chest wound. While waiting for the medics to evacuate him, Pyne smoked a cigarette. His men saw smoke come out of the hole in his chest each time he inhaled. He was evacuated and did survive. Lieutenant Hassenzahl took command.

The town of Opheusden was pounded continually with mortar and artillery fire, and there was more skirmishing with the German infantry. Company C was reduced to new commander Lt. Al Hassenzahl and 26 men in a day.

Sergeant Bill Knight of that company lost three weapons that day. Two rifles were struck by bullets, and a third was disabled by shrapnel. Another shell fragment lodged in the metal at the top of his bayonet scabbard. Miraculously Bill was not wounded by any of the flying metal.

Ray C. Allen's 401st Glider Inf. Bn. was brought up from the Veghel area to assist in relief of the 506. Colonel Allen's force was frequently used as a fire brigade within the division and seldom received due recognition for their heavy fighting.

Withdrawal

Allen met with his longtime friend Col. Robert Sink, who wanted him to take up positions right where the 506 was currently holding. Allen refused, stating that Opheusden itself held no strategic importance. Sink was concerned with the heavy losses his regiment had sustained in holding the town and didn't want to give up the real estate. Sink threatened to court-martial Allen, but cooler heads prevailed and backed Allen up. After all, the divisional mission at the time was to defend the corridor

On the Dike
Parachute infantrymen from 2/506 in position on the dike facing the Neder Rhine between Opheusden and Randwijk in October 1944. *US Army*

A small funeral service near Nijmegen for Col. H.R. Johnson. *Duggins*

and the highway between Arnhem and Nijmegen. Opheusden was far west of there and indeed held no strategic value in itself.

A plan was agreed on to form the 401 in a new line, 1,200yd east of the current line. The 1/ and 3/506 would then fall back through the 401.

When the battalions withdrew that night, Don Burgett of A/506 was left behind with several men and some machine guns, to act as rear guard. As the last of the battalion troops moved past, Burgett got a real "lonely feeling." Lieutenant Tony Borelli was in charge of the rearguard group, and at dawn, Burgett and friends kept asking, "Can we go now, lieutenant?"

Lieutenant Borelli was a cool character, well-liked by his men. He kept saying, "A little while longer."

At daylight, the group packed-up their weapons and hiked to the rear. En route, they passed near a large enemy force who must have thought they

Two Buddies on the Island, October, 1944
The man at left wears a resurrected M42 jumpsuit. The trooper at right wears the then-current M43 combat suit.

Krochka's caption indicates both men died a week later on a patrol. *Krochka*

were prisoners or their own troops. No shots were exchanged. Shortly thereafter, a massive German attack, by a battalion driving toward Nijmegen, came from the west. The 1/506, fighting from an apple orchard, helped repulse the group. A large number of Germans also entered a gap between companies of the 401, and scores were ambushed with little loss to the Americans.

Also that morning, Lieutenant Hassenzahl's 26-man company maneuvered against the rest of the German battalion, who were reported in a nearby woods. Sergeant Mariano Sanchez, "who had eyes like an eagle," called fire onto Germans in an open field, from the battalion's 81mm mortars. He then directed the mortars to walk fire through the woods. Sanchez received the Silver Star for this action but was killed at Bastogne. The Germans in the woods realized they were trapped and saw elements of the 327 coming up from the other direction.

As Hassenzahl's company approached the woods, Lieutenant Hatfield, leading half the group, lost contact. Corporal Harold Forshee, the lead scout, was shot dead. But dozens of Germans began coming out of the woods with no helmets and hands

on their heads. Hatfield fired his .45 at them and they ran back into the woods. Eventually, they came back out to surrender. Sergeant Bill Knight had admonished the lieutenant not to shoot at them, and a

Guarding the Dike
A classic photo of a dike position near Randwijk. The troopers are from 2/506. *Krochka*

Rhodes and Sharp, F/501

Two members of 3rd Platoon, F/501 man a 1919A4 LMG on the dike near the windmill west of Heteren in October 1944. A small road ran perpendicular to the dike here. At left is Emerson Rhodes, who recalls that his large mesh helmet net was then out of style in the 501. At right is Taylor Sharp. *Krochka*

surrender of nearly 250 Germans was accomplished.

Knight confiscated a whistle that one prisoner kept blowing, and another German was found in possession of a British commando knife, engraved with the name "Capt. Harold Van Antwerp." Van Antwerp had parachuted into Normandy as CO of G/506. He had been found dead on DZ D. This prisoner who was found with his knife was taken aside and shot. Hassenzahl felt, "This may or may not have been the right thing to do, as the knife could have changed hands four times or more since Nor-

The large windmill behind the dike between Randwijk-Heteren was easily identified by the large shell hole in one side. Here, Walter Craley of 501 demolitions sits with his back to the dike. *Prinerano*

Above, above right and below right
A paratrooper of the 501 bicycles past the clock tower in Heteren. It was from this tower (which was battered by numerous German bullets and shells) that David Smith of the HQ/501 S-2 section observed German movements across the dike. He was awarded a Bronze Star for his efforts. *Krochka*

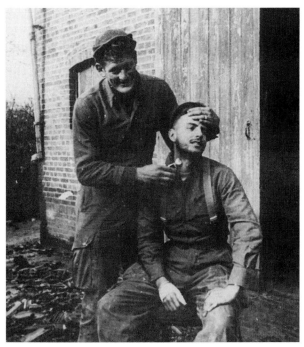

Quick Shave
One of the typical barn-like garages behind the dike was photographed near Heteren by John Primerano of HQ/501. A trooper named "Keith" is trimming the whiskers of Walter Craley. Craley was among the victims of the truck-mine explosion outside the Bastogne seminary in January, 1945. *Primerano.*

mandy." Another 40–50 dead Germans lay in the field near the woods, victims of the mortar barrage called-in by Sergeant Sanchez.

Three Troopers Ambush a Company

That night, 1st Sgt. Fred Bahlau, S/Sgt. Ben Hiner, and Lt. John Weisenberger of HQ/3 506 walked through German lines, returning to the Opheusden railroad station to recover some battalion baggage. All three were armed with Thompson submachine guns, and they planned to spend the night at the station. Bahlau spotted a company-size group of Germans approaching in the dark, but the group veered left and cut across the track, heading for Opheusden. Hiner went up into a window of the house on the left. Weisenberger entered a barn to the right. At a given signal, they opened fire on the flank of the enemy company, which was passing them broadside, at a range of 100yd. A German machine gun returned fire, knocking shingles off the roof of the station, but the bulk of the enemy unit kept moving ahead as if bent on a mission. After some grenades had been hurled at the enemy force, the last 40 men in the group dropped back and came in, surrendering to the three Americans. An unknown number had been killed. The prisoners were marched to the rear.

Fred Bahlau's Second Silver Star

The next day, Maj. Jim Harwick was riding in a jeep with the driver and Lieutenant Heggeness when the jeep was ambushed by a German machine gun. The driver was killed, and the jeep crashed into a water-filled ditch. The officers escaped and Harwick supplied Sergeant Bahlau with another jeep and driver, directing them to return to the ambush site and recover his map case, which had been left in the shot-up vehicle.

In a daring daylight move, Bahlau and driver sped down the road, located the shot-up jeep, retrieved the map case and the body of Harwick's driver, and returned successfully. Bahlau was awarded his second Silver Star Medal for this incident.

Probing into Opheusden

In the following days and weeks, the west perimeter of the Island was largely taken over by the 401 and the 327. Although Opheusden was back in German hands, numerous American patrols probed into the town almost daily.

Sergeant John R. Gacek was seriously wounded and left behind on one of the patrols. The next day, a patrol returning to that location found Gacek still alive. He was evacuated, but died. The C/401 launched a patrol across the Neder Rhine in rafts to reconnoiter and look for a prisoner. The patrol was uneventful and returned empty handed. Another effort to cross in a raft by Lt. Fred J. Rau and Chinese-American S/Sgt. Gilbert M. Chinn was ambushed while in the water; both of the glider troopers were killed.

Tex McMorries and the Battle for the Dike

When 2/ and 3/501 relieved British troops on the Neder Rhine dike between Heteren and Driel, the Brits were glad to go. The sector had been quiet because the Brits had enjoyed an unspoken truce with the Germans—a reciprocal no-shooting policy.

The Germans held two brick kilns down near the water and had their backs to the Rhine. But several hundred yards of pasture separated the shoreline where the kilns were located from the road on the main dike. The landward shoulder of this main dike became the front line for troopers of the 501. They dug their foxholes just below the shoulder of the road and could hear Germans digging and talking 30ft away, on the opposite slope of the dike. Only the road atop the dike separated the opposing sides, and the Americans stirred up a fight as soon as they arrived. As a result, the quiet period ended.

A concerted effort began to drive the Germans from the opposite slope of the dike. The Americans found that their artillery could not be effectively employed against reverse slope defenses less than 50ft away. Someone tied a bunch of boot laces together, attached a fragmentation grenade to one end of the long string, pulled the pin, then tossed it over. This prevented the grenade from rolling to the bottom of

The Slob Farm
The Slob Farm on the canal near Zetten, Holland, as it looked in 1944. This was used as POW interrogation site. The building has since been torn down.

Gone Without a Trace
In 1989, the DeHaartogs showed the author the former site of the Slob Farm. It used to be on the bank of this canal.

the reverse slope before exploding. Next, it was realized that a length of parachute suspension line would more conveniently serve the same purpose. Finally, someone realized that WP grenades would be ideal for burning the Germans out of their holes. At dusk on the evening of 5 October, a jeepload of WP grenades and salvaged parachutes arrived, and the 501 resolved that there would be no Germans on the dike by morning.

In G/501, Tex McMorries and Bob Baldwin (as usual) had drawn a diagram of the troop situation in the area and had concluded that because of the inflexible nature of the front line on the dike, the safest place to be would be in the midst of the enemy front line. When the troops began tossing their WP grenades across, two G/501 men crossed the dike. Tex, firing his LMG from the hip, was joined by Private Rowland. Tex shot one German in his hole, then jumped into it and began firing the machine gun to the right along the enemy slope and then to the left. Then he would duck as the enemy troops on either side returned fire. As he and Baldwin had expected, this caused chaos in the German line. Tex spotted a sizable group of German reinforcements rushing up on the right flank and sent Rowland back across to the friendly side to alert the men on the US line.

Tex had been blown off his feet by German concussion grenades while originally crossing over the dike road, and fragments had entered his lung. Even so, he stayed most of the night on the enemy side of the dike, firing periodically to either flank. In the wee hours of the morning, two Germans crept up and leaped into Tex's hole with knives. He succeeded in killing both of them. Just before dawn, Tex returned to the south side of the dike, bringing his LMG along. The surviving Germans on the dike fell

back to the brick factory before daylight, and the dike belonged to the 501.

A later count of German dead on the reverse slope and in the field nearby revealed 26 German bodies, many killed by Tex McMorries. Once again, Tex was written up for a DSC but would never receive the medal.

The Diary

For the next several days, long-range warfare ensued, with the enemies taking potshots at each other across the pasture. Tex and Baldwin each got several chances at a German officer as he moved

Chow Time
The I/502 chow line at Dodewaard, Holland, October 1944. *Molsberry*

Company COs
Company commanders of 3/502 in Holland: Champ Baker of I Company (with first-aid kit on his helmet) and Robert Jones and Frank Lillyman of HQ/3 (standing), in Elst, Holland. *Author's collection*

IPW Teams
Lieutenant Alphonse Gion (left) was an excellent IPW officer for Col. Robert Sink's 506. The IPW teams were a part of each regiment in the ETO and performed a vital function in obtaining unit identifications, troop dispositions and strengths, order of battle, and other facts from German prisoners. Many of the interrogators were first- or second-generation immigrants from Europe, and many were Jewish. The team usually consisted of one or two officers (a captain and a lieutenant) and four enlisted men (usually a master sergeant, a staff sergeant, and two technicians). During the first week of the Holland invasion, all of the regiments had an ample supply of prisoners and myriad German units were identified from the disintegrating German Fifteenth Army. *Palys*

among enemy positions near the river. "Just when you thought you had him, he would do the unexpected," Tex later said. "His timing was unbelievable, and he had no doubt fought in many battles."

Finally, observers reported that there was no activity in and near the brick factory. The last of the enemy had evidently crossed to the north shore of the Neder Rhine.

That night, a patrol worked its way down to the factory and found it deserted, except for German bodies. Near one body was a diary, with daily entries dating back to the 17 September invasion. Tex recovered this book and turned it in to S-2 for translation.

Shortly after WWII ended, Tex returned to Texas with the dead man's diary. It had belonged to a lieutenant from Jena, named Kurt Martin from the SS Von Rautenfeld Reg. Inside the cover of the diary was the home address of Martin's wife in Jena. Tex wrote a letter to that address, presumably to Martin's widow. He was amazed to receive in return a letter in English from Martin himself. He had not been killed, and his diary had evidently dropped from his pocket near another man in the brick factory before Martin escaped across the river.

The abridged text of the letter appears below:

3 May, 1947

Dear Mr. Melton:

When I came home to my family after some time, my wife gave me your letter. I was very surprised but at the same time very glad . . . I shall write to you today, as I am interested to know how my address came to your knowledge. After all you

write in your letter, I am no doubt the man of whom you speak. I was in September and October in the bridgehead near Arnhem and have commanded same as last German officer. On October 10, I was gravely wounded. In the evening of the same day I was brought across the Rhine in the military hospital of Appeldoorn, for the hospital of Arnhem was already overcrowded. The next day I had to undergo an operation. For five days I was between life and death. Finally, however, I got away with life. In February 1945, I had to return to the front and was taken prisoner by the Americans in Germany in May. After my release, I returned to my family in September '46.

So I have been away from home for 7-1/2 years. My children had grown up in the meantime. You are right, the war was hard for all of us, but I have only done my duty as has every decent soldier for his country. We are glad that the war is over and that we can work in peace . . . we hope to receive soon a long-lasting peace because only in that way can the people march into a better future. We have had to suffer very much as a consequence of the war, and it will take a long time until we can live better. But in spite of all this, we will not lose our courage but we will work and help to get a good agreement between all the nations . . .

I am sending you best regards as comrades, and I should be glad to hear from you soon. Please tell me if you want to know further details from me then.

Sincerely yours,

MARTIN

Thus began one of the most remarkable pen-pal relationships to develop between former enemies of WWII. The warriors exchanged photos of their children and informed each other of the situation at the dike battle, each from their own perspective.

Among other things, Tex learned that Martin had been the elusive target he had missed with his machine gun. He also learned that after the big battle in which the Germans were driven from the dike, Lieutenant Martin had sent English-speaking patrols up to the dike each night in darkness. They had listened to the 501 troopers talking and had learned the name "McMorries" was responsible for the death of so many of their comrades. Martin informed Tex that he had offered a high decoration as a reward for the killing or capture of McMorries.

Holding Period

With the Germans driven across the Neder Rhine in the Heteren area, a long period of holding began. Snipers fired across the river from ranges near 700yd. Artillery and mortar fire were exchanged on a regular basis. The 101st would spend nearly two full months, the bulk of October and November on the Island. A total of 73 days was spent on the front lines in Holland, and the Germans were unable to dislodge the tip of the Market-Garden salient.

The flanks of the dike position offered little concealment for a possible buildup to destroy the US bridgehead, and the only other alternative would have been an amphibious crossing of the Neder Rhine. Although this was a remote possibility, numerous patrols crossed the river at night to find out if the Germans were indeed massing for such a push and to find out what units were opposing the division across the river. Although some of these patrols got into shoot-outs on the enemy shore, they returned with little information.

"I Got My Teeth Into It"

Trooper E. O. Parmeley was an original member of F/502 and is among those who jumped in Normandy in June 1994 to observe the 50th anniversary of D-day. He recalled the inspection depicted in the photo, in the *Chappie Hall* newsletter #11 (19 March, 1969):

After we had been in Holland for about a month, our second battalion was assembled for an inspection by Gen. Taylor. Morale was low, we were all tired, each company looked like a platoon. I would say we were a sad looking lot. Well, Gen. Taylor, on previous occasions had remarked that what we wanted was to get our teeth into this war and in our Bn., some of the men were always yelling, "You got to get your teeth into it!" Gen. Taylor arrived in a green jacket, no webbing of any kind on, but in his hip pocket he had a .45 with just the butt sticking out. I think he was there to boost our morale for as he came down the ranks he spoke to most of the men or asked such questions as, "Know how to use that rifle?" or to the bazooka man, "Have you hit any tanks with that, soldier?" There was a man in D Company, I believe, who had no teeth. His false ones were in his pocket. When Gen. Taylor asked him how he was, he said "Well, General, Sir, I got my teeth into it!" and then proceeded to give him his best Colgate smile. There were a lot of laughs and this story spread around. It was a terrific morale builder.

General Maxwell Taylor, CO of the 101st Airborne, inspected 2/502 in Holland, October 1944. Here, Taylor (center) is questioning a member of the 81mm mortar platoon. On the left (with vertical strap on helmet) is Capt. James Roy Martin, CO of HQ/2. At the extreme right is Major Thomas Sutliffe, the 2/502 executive officer.

Another Kind Of Heroism

Since the Germans had vacated the brick factory east of Heteren, a squad of American troopers manned the building at all times. One night, a squad

Return of the Incredible Patrol
A view inside the Slob Farm (a POW interrogation site) soon after the return of the 501's Incredible Patrol, showing Lt. Werner Meier (right) with some of the captives. Hauptsturmfuhrer Walter Gartner, CO of 1/502 SS Artillery Reg. (part of II SS Panzer Korps), is visible with M43 cap and fur collar at left. Joe Pangerl, the 502's IPW officer motored up to see the large group of prisoners. Pangerl was stationed at Dodewaard at the time he took this photo. *Pangerl*

from H/501 occupied the building. A small fire was built inside the factory to heat water for coffee and to generate some warmth. It was difficult to get the fire going well, so J. C. Mann, a Normandy veteran, tossed some gasoline onto the fire. But the handle of the canteen cup bearing the flammable liquid caught on his sleeve and gas spilled all over the front of his field jacket. Mann burst into flames and another trooper received lesser burns.

Mann was badly burned over much of his body. This had happened near dawn, and the men in the outpost found that injecting Mann with morphine was doing nothing to ease his agony, because of the nature of his injuries.

By daylight, the situation was intolerable, but the men realized that they were supposed to remain in the position until relieved. They also realized that moving across the 300yd pasture between the factory and dike in daylight was almost suicidal. Leonard Morris called on the radio and reached S/Sgt. John McMullen at the CP, explaining the situation. McMullen conferred with the company commander, Capt. Lytle Hilton, who relayed orders not to attempt to evacuate the burned soldier until nightfall, as the movement would attract artillery fire from across the river.

Ignoring orders, Morris said over the radio, "We're coming in. Tell the old man to have an ambulance ready when we get there."

Morris placed Mann in a fireman's carry and began the journey back across the pasture, fully exposed to enemy observation from across the river. He had to pause to rest numerous times, but the Germans never fired. Perhaps they felt admiration for this courageous act, maybe even compassion for the wounded man.

Sergeant McMullen told Morris "The old man wants to see you," shortly after Mann was turned over to the medics.

Morris entered Captain Hilton's office and received a blistering chewing-out, but no further action was taken against him. Men sometimes do what they feel they have to do.

Long-Range Warfare
The long-range warfare alluded to earlier was characterized by hide and seek and sniping activities. The cunning Germans had anticipated this and had prepared for it.

In one tall house behind the dike, an upstairs window was visible from across the river. The Germans had hung a white bed sheet on the wall across from the open window before they retreated across the river. A trooper standing in the room later, thinking he was safe because of the great distance to enemy lines, was silhouetted against the sheet.

Glen A. Derber had been an NRA rifle champion before the war. For some reason, the Army placed him in the 2/501's LMG Platoon. Glen didn't like the machine gun. The precise, well-aimed rifle shot was what he understood and excelled at, so Glen was allowed to carry an 03-A3 Springfield bolt-action rifle. Up on the dike near Heteren, he was able to excel at long-distance sniping by using that weapon.

Glen's diary excerpts from that period give a fascinating insight into some of his activities on the dike:

I borrowed a pair of field glasses and started some sniping activities with my '03. I saw a Kraut about 600 yards or so away, lying outside his hole in the warm sun, so I tried a shot. He didn't move. I guessed the bullet couldn't have gotten to him, so I set my sights up to 700 yards and tried again. He scrambled to his feet and ducked into his foxhole, then looked around, wondering who was shooting at him. The next time I fired, he ducked into his hole again. When he came up to look again, he had his rifle. I tried another shot and he went down again. I checked with the field glasses after each shot, and when I looked after my last shot, he was aiming at me!

I got ready to fire again, and a bullet cracked above my head. It seemed pretty wide to me and I was all for this game. This was something I could enjoy, for I had great confidence in my rifle and my ability to use it. The next shot I fired must have hit him in the head for he bounded out of his hole as if by reflex action and went tumbling head over heels down the side of the dike. Some other Kraut came over to take a look at him, and I scared him off with a shot.

I had a lot of fun that afternoon, wounding two more and two probables . . . The following day I got in some more sniping, with no definite results.

There was the usual exchange or mortar and artillery barrages. The nights were getting cool now, and dense ground fog would move in on us . . .

I was sent back to the CP to get some rest . . . I didn't like the boredom back there, so I would go up on the dike when I got a chance and do a little sniping. I just loved to fire my rifle.

Well it seems the Germans had caught on to this sniping too, and they had a well-concealed sniper at work on a certain section of our lines. Two men had been hit in the head when they stuck their heads up over the dike to look around. I was itching for a rifle fight this day, so I thought I'd try to find him and have a little duel. I tried all the tricks I knew. I'd push my helmet up at one place and then sneak up near a place where I had background against which I couldn't be easily seen. Then I'd poke the glasses through some grass and look around the landscape, trying to locate that sniper. He must have had a powerful telescope or something because he would never shoot at just a helmet stuck up in view. And I can thank my lucky stars that he wasn't too good a shot, because here I was looking through the glasses, when all of a sudden a bullet hit the sod directly across the road from me. Six inches higher would have put it right through my head.

Colonel Johnson's Death

On 8 October, Col. Howard R. "Jumpy" Johnson of the 501 was behind the main dike west of Heteren, inspecting the front-line of D/501. With him were a number of officers, including Captains Pelham and Snodgrass. Intermittent artillery shells came in from across the river, but the colonel was loath to take cover in front of his troops. When a very close 88mm round came in, the other officers hit the deck, but Jumpy remained upright as the shell exploded near him.

The colonel went down with numerous wounds and was rushed by jeep to the aid station, then moved by ambulance to a field hospital, still alive and conscious.

Major Francis E. Carrel, the 501's regimental surgeon, examined the colonel on an operating table. He first examined a wound on the front of Johnson's right shoulder. As Carrel cleaned that wound, Johnson said, "Doc, it's my back that hurts."

Deadeye
Glen A. Derber of the LMG platoon HQ/2 501, is shown sighting down a 1919 A-4 light machinegun. Glen engaged in long range sniping with an 03-A3 rifle on the island in October, 1944. Derber

Rolling the colonel part ways over, Carrel could see a gaping entry hole above the right hip, near his lower back. The shell splinter had gone through sideways and not quite exited near the lower left abdominal area. Carrel was able to remove a piece of jagged steel 1in wide and about 5in long. There was massive damage to the colonel's spleen and bowels. Johnson died on the operating table.

Johnson's death sent a shock wave through his entire regiment. He had been a link with home and was closely identified with as the image and identity of the entire unit. Most of his men were surprised. Surprised that their larger-than-life leader could actually be killed. As Critchell wrote: "To outlive him seemed strange." Lieutenant Colonel Julian Ewell ascended to regimental command.

Colonel Johnson's Funeral

Colonel Johnson was undoubtedly one of the immortal leaders of the 101st Airborne and will live on in the annals of the division as long as its history is preserved. The colorful colonel was one-of-a-kind.

Half a dozen members of G/501 went to Nijmegen for the colonel's funeral service. (Johnson's body was later returned to the States and now rests in Arlington National Cemetery.)

One of the men on the honor guard told me that they fired tracers from their rifles in the 21-gun salute, as "Jumpy would have liked it."

Colonel Johnson's burial is best described in the haunting poem written by Melton "Tex" McMorries of G/501:

Leonard Swartz and Georgie Dietz
Leonard Swartz, regimental mail clerk of the 502, with Georgie Dietz, a nine-year-old from Andelst, Holland, in early October. Georgie was later killed by a German bomb while playing in the street. *Musura*

• • •

Geronimo is Dead

This is the beautiful land he played a leading role in liberating,

The once quiet, peaceful land of Holland.

Its orchards are scarred and injured.

Most of its neat little homes lie as only crumpled brick.

The smooth farmland over which his little Geronimos moved on toward Arnhem

Lies flooded.

His body lies far below the heights he lived on:

For Geronimo was king of the paratroopers;

None hit the silk as he.

This was not his first invasion, but it was his last.

Holing Up on the Island
Lieutenant Emzy Gaydon, A/502, in a log-roofed bunker on the Island, in October 1944. *Locasto*

He could have stayed in some other place, but it's more peaceful where he now lies.

One hundred and thirty odd times he'd felt the cold chill of the prop—

Never again for him.

Colonel Johnson's parachute days are through.

Lean, tough paratroopers of his Geronimo band stand at attention amid the cold grey crosses.

Death to them was no stranger—

Yet burial was.

So that's what they do with the ones that fall; we thought they just lay where they fell.

Farther in the field grey soldiers of another army stand as ghosts to mock the dead.

They are the PWs, the grave diggers,

Who must love their job.

He shouldn't be lonesome here.

He has so much company, acres and acres, beneath the
damp cold earth.

They should understand his faint whispers, men of the
101st and 82nd Airborne.

Yet somehow he looks lonesome.

The Chaplain has said his word, the volley is fired, the
generals file past his grave.

Now the other ranks file off slowly.

They pass among the rows, careful not to disturb the sleeping.

Case, Baldwin, Serawatka, Kane, Parrish, McMorries;

Each pauses at his grave, gazes in at the camouflaged
parachute the king sleeps in.

It looks cold down there; wonder if he'll keep warm.

Slowly the moving picture camera clicks away, recording
the procedure;

But never could it record the feelings of the tough men
who pass the grave.

No pity, no tears.

They had lived too long for that, saw death too often.

Three of the men who pass that way, their guns have
killed over thirty in one day.

Somehow it's wrong.

Maybe a year ago it would have been easy to figure.

But now it's too late; you only know that as soon as the
last man of the honor guard files past you will go back to
the line and the only life you do understand, war.

No, he is not going back.

Propellor blasts have died away.

His parachute days are through.

Yes, there will be a telegram;

Oh! but if she only knew.

The sun is getting lower, the words they speak are few.

Yet each trooper's thought lingers on Geronimo,

King of the parachute crew.

•••

Geronimo is Dead
This classic portrait of the CO of the 501, Colonel Howard
R. Johnson, was made during the regiment's training in
the States. Johnson's death sent shock waves through the
501. *Amburgey*

Mission Of Mercy

On the night of 22–23 October the largest of two
rescue operations was launched across the Neder
Rhine, to evacuate the last British paratroopers who
had survived the Arnhem slaughter. With help from
Dutch civilians who hid the men in houses and
barns for over a month, with little food, the British
troopers had hidden in the vicinity of Renkum-
Doorwerth. Most of the rescue detail was recruited
from E/506, but G/501 men and members of several
other companies were also involved.

The rescuers followed white engineer tapes to
the shore and were ferried across the river by Canadian engineers. Bofors guns fired diversionary tracers, and a V sign was flashed from the far shore with
a red flashlight.

On the enemy shore, firing was forbidden. The
rescuers moved forward with knives at the ready.

Tex McMorries of G/501 was involved in one of
the crossings, and in the larger operation, about 130
Brit paras and a few Allied flyers were rescued. Tex
wrote:

The survivors were starved and exhausted to
the point that only a thread separated them from insanity and for some, the thread broke. But still, they
had the pride of being a trooper, and I think this

carried them the extra hour and day that salvaged them from destruction and insanity.

The Incredible Patrol

Near the end of October, S-2/501 launched a patrol that crossed the Neder Rhine below Renkum, in darkness, to capture a prisoner. Lieutenant Hugo S. Sims had conceived the patrol, which in fact returned with 31 prisoners. Sims had been disappointed in the efforts of various companies to cross and return with a prisoner, so he requested to lead this patrol himself, "as a stimulus to the battalions." Colonel Ewell initialed his approval on the written request, and Sims selected six of his best men to make the patrol.

Sergeant Peter Frank, a French- and German-speaking soldier who came from Belgium, would accompany Sgt. Bill Canfield, Robert O. Nicolai, Roland J. Wilbur, and Frederick J. "Ted" Becker.

The patrol members blackened their faces, wore wool caps, and carried Tommyguns and .45cal pistols, except Wilbur, who was known to shoot for the head with his M-1.

Using aerial photos, Sims had selected landmarks in advance with the patrol reaching each one at a pre-planned time. Occupying a house on the Utrecht-Arnhem highway, the patrol stayed there for most of the following day, capturing numerous German soldiers who entered the dwelling unaware that it was occupied by Americans. Later, a truck containing 13 SS artillerymen was captured with all aboard, and the troopers prepared to drive back to the river with their growing bag of captives. An SS captain arrived in a Schwimwagen to look for his missing truckload of men. He was added to the collection. The group drove toward the river until the truck broke down. Then the group marched briskly, passing other Germans who thought the Americans were prisoners.

The German prisoners complained about the brisk marching speed, and the SS captain bolted away into the woods but was apprehended and returned to the group by Nicolai, who administered a few swift kicks to the captain's posterior. Passing in a marching formation right through the town of Renkum, the group cleaned out a few German outposts on the riverbank, then blinked their signal for pickup to the friendly shore. Rowboats came across, manned by men who had volunteered because they were strong swimmers.

Ed Hallo of A/501 was among them and recalled that two troopers manned each boat. On the return trip, two prisoners rode in the center of each boat, rowing, while the Americans fore and aft guarded them. Eventually, all 31 prisoners and the patrol members arrived safely on the south shore.

Only two (warning) shots had been fired on the entire patrol. The prisoners were taken south to the "Slob Farm" along a canal northeast of Zetten for interrogation. Lieutenant Werner Meier had his work cut out for him in questioning this big batch, and Lt. Joseph Pangerl, the 502 IPW officer, drove up from Dodewaard to view the catch.

This patrol received widespread publicity throughout the ETO and won Sims a DSC and a promotion to captain. The other patrol members received the Silver Star.

Life At Dodewaard

Southeast of Opheusden, elements of the 502 held the southwest flank of the division line near Dodewaard. Action in the area was mostly limited to patrolling, and many men were killed or wounded by the thousands of German land mines planted in the area.

A press photographer visited this sector during October and told Schuyler Jackson that he wanted to get a great action photo. At a loss for what to do, the men decided to "stage" a picture. They planted some C-2 with a remote detonator in a nice pile of mud and positioned one trooper to the rear of it. The trooper struck a pose with his weapon at the ready and at a given signal, the charge was detonated. The photographer snapped a still photo of the explosion and the photo was later published in many books, newspapers, and magazines. The caption said the picture showed an American paratrooper near Arnhem, advancing under 88mm fire. It was hailed as one of the great action shots of WWII.

A Tragic Accident

On 22 October at Dodewaard, Sgt. George Sheppard of the 502 demolitions platoon was unwinding wire from a German Riegel mine. Nearby was a large pile of the mines that had been recently recovered from the surrounding terrain. The mine in his hand exploded; this touched off the entire pile. Lt. Richard Daily and all present, except two, were killed immediately. Oresti "Rusty" Quirici had a metal-covered bible in his chest pocket that stopped a piece of shrapnel, but Rusty was blown into the nearby canal. One of his buddies, Cpl. Robert Brigham, lived until the following day, then died. Quirici, the sole survivor of the blast visited Holland in September, 1994, with his metal-covered Bible. Also killed in the blast were Ed Ambrose, Joe St. Clair, Warren Grunert, and Joseph Hill.

A Little Humor

Lieutenant Ed Wierzbowski of H/502 had survived the nightmarish fight near the canal with Joe Mann outside of Best. In the late 1960's Lieutenant "Whizbow," as he was nicknamed, sent a humorous story to the *Chappie Hall Newsletter* (the 502 veterans' newsletter), recalling an incident at Dodewaard:

. . . the Power that be decided that the boys were out of condition, having spent so much time on the front lines. The order came down that H company would have a period of exercise. Naturally the assignment was mine. At any rate, as I called the company to attention, out of the corner of my eye, I saw a couple of my boys walking across the farmyard with two Dutch girls. (I won't mention their names, but they are well remembered, I can assure you). Coming from the barn, where they had spent the night teaching the girls my name (that's what they told me) . . . so there we are, the company at attention and me waiting for these characters to join the ranks. When suddenly the girls began to shout (bowing and grinning all the time) "Gut Morgen Lieutenant Chickashit, Gut Morgen Lieutenant Chickashit." They were grinning so much that it broke everyone up as well as the P.T. session.

The Death Of Ben Shaub

Another prime example of the wasted lives resulting from the numerous land mines sown near Dodewaard is to be found in the screening patrol launched toward the canal below Opheusden by F/502.

The patrol reached a Dutch house near the canal embankment and stayed in position for several hours, calling in reports on a radio. Near the house was a minefield that had been swept by the 326; red flags marked the numerous mines that were located but not yet removed.

Looking into the basement of the house through an open door revealed a three-step stairwell leading to a wooden table. Stuck into the top of the table was a beautiful Nazi dagger.

"Don't even go down there," Joe Pistone cautioned his men—it was almost certain that the stairs or the dagger itself were booby-trapped to explode.

Ignoring the warning, Ben Shaub, who had won the Silver Star in Normandy for his heroic decimation of a German artillery battery, walked onto the front lawn of the house. There was a loud explosion, and the men looked out to see Shaub lying on the lawn with one foot blown off below the ankle. Leaves were fluttering down from the trees from the concussion of the blast.

Without hesitation for his own safety, Pvt. Andrew Hemrock walked out onto the lawn and grabbed Shaub under both arms. He began dragging him back.

Another explosion rocked the area, and Hemrock fell wounded with an identical wound. The second blast had also inflicted a critical wound to Shaub's head and upper body.

A medic named Knapp, who had replaced Baker after Normandy braved the mined lawn, walking out and giving both of the wounded men shots of morphine.

General Taylor Visits the Currahee Regiment
General Taylor chats with a 2/506 medic during Holland inspection. The tall officer with hands clasped behind his back is Colonel Sink. Dick Winters is to the immediate left of Sink. *Photo courtesy Winters*

The medic received help from four or five men who dragged the wounded troopers back to a clearing where there were no mines. A half hour later, more troopers arrived with stretchers and carried the wounded men out. As Hemrock was leaving, he lay on the stretcher, smiling and twirling a Dutch derby hat on a bayonet blade. Hemrock's indomitable spirit was an inspiration to his buddies, but Ben Shaub, the hero of Normandy, was dying.

Withdrawal and the First Shower in 72 Days

The 501 had just left its dike positions when the Germans placed an aerial bomb in the dike at the curve east of Coffin Corner. They blew open the dike and the current of the Neder Rhine sent water rushing under the railroad viaduct and flooding the land behind the dike as far west as Opheusden. Much of the area was under water for over six months, until Canadian engineers repaired the dike with bulldozers in 1945.

The 101st Div. was being withdrawn to go into reserve at the new base of the First Allied Airborne Army at Reims, France. Assorted divisions and airborne battalions from throughout the European Theater of Operations (ETO) were being consolidated there.

The area east of Opheusden was already flooding when Don Burgett's buddies were finally evacuated. They had been issued empty 5gal gas cans to use as emergency flotation devices, and were perched on rooftops "like chickens on a roost," when Canadian engineers picked them up in boats.

Don and friends were taken to a monastery equipped with a field shower and had their first shower in 72 days before leaving the Island for good.

Thanks for a Job Well Done
Lieutenant General Sir Miles Dempsey, commander of the British Second Army in Holland, addressed a contingent of troopers from sub-units throughout the division, thanking them for a job well done. *Krochka*

Market-Garden In Retrospect— One Trooper's Summary

After leaving Holland, Dick Ladd of the 502's S-2 section wrote:

Market-Garden—indeed an imaginative strategy . . . an abortive end run around the Siegfried Line—could have worked. We, the Airborne, were the "magic carpet" over which the British Second Army was to roll. Unfortunately, a combination of poor geographical planning (operation predicated on one sole corridor highway), and poor British tactics . . . Regarding the latter, the British Army had no dash nor vigor in moving with alacrity or smashing and bypassing resistance. When a lead tank or armored car was hit or "brewed-up," their armored units seldom seemed to react or maneuver the way American armor or German panzer elements re-

Flooded Foxholes
Sergeant Ed Benecke of A/377 in his dugout near Elst, Holland, in November 1944. The Germans had blown the dike near Coffin Corner, and water was starting to seep into the foxholes, causing the men to build up higher with crates and discarded materials to get above the new water table. *Benecke*

sponded. So much for learning much in the desert from Rommel. British Infantry—excellent fighters, tough to dislodge if they didn't want to go. However, I suspect that many priggish officers and class-conscious ways mitigated against effective relationships with their men. Consequence was the British Second Army languishing in a dead-end corridor until early February 1945. A lot of troops, gas, and material expended at the expense of a breakthrough to the Rhine by George Patton's Third Army . . . but Monty had his way with Ike.

Chapter Ten

Mourmelon Interlude

The new base of the First Allied Airborne Army's American troops was in the area of Reims, France. The 101st Airborne, along with the 82nd Airborne, were stationed outside of Reims to recuperate and re-fit after being withdrawn from Holland. Numerous replacements were to be absorbed into the existing units, and weapons were to be replaced along with other worn out equipment.

The 101st was situated in stone French Army barracks, which had more recently housed German panzer troops. Large murals of nude women had been painted on the walls of the mess hall by the former German tenants. One of the regimental chaplains deemed that the murals were morally unfit for the troops to gaze upon while eating and ordered them painted over. The stone billets of the 101st were in the town of Mourmelon le Grand. On the other side of Reims, the 82nd was stationed at Camp Suippes. Numerous other small, independent airborne units were also assembled near Reims.

The barracks' at Mourmelon had a toilet and sewage system of sorts, but this proved inadequate when an outbreak of dysentery suddenly afflicted dozens of troopers. The epidemic was caused by tainted food—some leftover turkey brought out of Holland and other mystery meat served at the new base camp. While a big football game was scheduled and awaited between the 502 and the 506 (The Champagne Bowl), some troops were sent on three-day passes to Paris. Other troops invaded the city of Reims, and the inevitable mayhem erupted when the Screaming Eagles clashed with 82nd All-Americans after consuming copious amounts of wine, co-

gnac, and other assorted spirits. Shots were fired, entire bars were temporarily commandeered by US paras, fights broke out, troopers swung from crystal chandeliers or made demonstration jumps from third floor balconies, MPs were attacked and disarmed, and a strict schedule was established to ensure that members of the 82nd and 101st went to town on different, alternating nights.

In his book *Those Devils In Baggy Pants*, Ross Carter of the 82nd Airborne wrote:

> When eventually we did get passes to Reims, the troopers took the town by storm. We left a shameful record for which I apologize to all Frenchmen, but I think part of the blame should be farmed out to the top brass. After all, old fighting men should not be treated like recruits. But maybe it would have happened anyway. I'm afraid that the people of Reims will henceforth judge the American way of life by our conduct. They would be wrong of course; but after all, most people form opinions on what they see and hear, and the citizens of Reims saw plenty. It is unfortunate that most of them didn't understand what they heard.

The two-buckle combat boots had been forced upon the jumpers before they went to Holland. This became an extra sore spot in late 1944, when the troopers came out of combat in Holland to discover rear echelon, non-jumping personnel walking around wearing jump boots. Most straight-leg officers were also wearing jump boots.

Don Burgett recalled:

Divisional CP, Mourmelon le Grand
This brick building was the 101st's HQ for almost three full weeks. Ed Hallo of A/501 had the detail to lower the flag on the roof each evening. *Benecke*

We couldn't get jump boots, and we were the paratroopers. A guy in my company [Slick Hoenschedit] saw a major in Reims wearing jump boots. This hit him at the wrong time, and he proceeded to just beat the hell out of this major. He said, "You non-jumping, rear-echelon son of a bitch! It's 'cause of people like you that we can't get jump boots."

After he beat the major up, Slick took a knife and cut the boots off the major's feet. MPs were called, and they arrested Slick. Lieutenant Borelli came to the stockade, vouched for Slick, and got him released, telling him to go straight back to camp. But Slick stopped off in a bar to have a quick drink en route back. Coming out the door, he came face to face with the same major, whose eyes were black and face all puffed-up. The major started screaming for MPs, but Slick took off running and escaped. That major later circulated wanted posters around the ETO, trying to locate Slick so he could bring charges against him.

The Unforeseen Counteroffensive

Ever since the humiliating sacking of his Seventh Army near Chambois, Hitler had contemplated a massive counteroffensive to turn the tide of the fighting in Europe. If a massive assault was hurled against a thinly held sector and could drive to Antwerp, capturing a coastal port, perhaps the catastrophic casualties would make the Allies sue for peace. Hitler also believed that the partnership between the US and the UK was tenuous and could be easily torn asunder by a massive German onslaught.

To this end, Hitler had overseen the rebuilding of many elite units that had been decimated in Normandy, including the 2nd and 116th Panzer Div., the Panzer Lehr Div., and the Panzers of the 1st, 2nd, and 12th SS Div. By late fall 1944, Hitler had quietly moved these rebuilt divisions and massive numbers of tanks and armor toward the weakest sector in the US front lines.

Operation Watch on Rhine would launch this powerful counter-thrust through the traditional German attack route of Ardennes, Belgium. Two green US infantry divisions held the north–south line from Elsenborn to the Schnee Eifel area—the 99th and 106th Div. Below them were two veteran divisions, battle weary from the drive across western Europe and the recent fighting around Aachen and the Hurtgen Forest, the 28th and 4th Div. Elements of the green 9th Armored Div., 14th Cavalry Group, and other small units were also on the line in the Ardennes front area.

By early December 1944, Hitler's target area was most definitely narrowed down to the Ardennes front, scene of his successful Blitz in 1940. Other factors—surprise, fog, and the worst weather of any western European winter since 1900—would all be of help to Hitler's counterattack. The quiet sector just west of the German frontier was about to explode.

The Battle of The Bulge Begins

Just before dawn on 16 December 1944, massive German artillery barrages heralded the opening of Hitler's Ardennes counteroffensive. Hitler's Sixth SS Panzer Army, mainly consisting of the 1st and II SS Panzer Corps followed the thundering barrage on the northern sector, with tanks and infantry swarming along the roads south of Elsnborn. The 99th Inf. Div., although inexperienced, held firm at the northern shoulder, soon joined by the 2nd Inf. Div. and then the 1st Inf. Div. They stopped cold the drive of the 12th SS in front of Elsenborn Ridge and massed artillery to kill hundreds of SS troopers at Dom Butgenbach. But just south of there, SS Lt. Col. Jochen Peiper's battlegroup of the 1st SS was driving madly westward, through Lanzerath, Honsfeld, Bullingen, then skirting south of the city of Malmedy. At the Baugnez crossroads, members of the 1st SS opened fire on a group of over 100 unarmed American

Rest and Recuperation

These 101st Airborne IPW officers left Holland for a brief recuperation period at Camp Mourmelon, France, late in 1944 (left to right): Loeffler, Al Gion, Vidor, Werner "Mike" Meier, Kipnis, Schwisow, and Pangerl. Werner Meier detected a sense of antagonism from his CO, Col. Howard Johnson, along with a lack of appreciation of the importance of the job the IPW teams had to do. He also felt that Johnson's ruthless attitude toward the enemy, which was transferred to many of his troops, contributed to more deaths—on both sides. After Johnson's tragic death in October 1944, Meier was able to work with Lieutenant Colonel Ewell, the new CO, in a better spirit of cooperation. Meier recalls several times asking that the troopers take more prisoners so he would have more material to work with to gain information. "Don't forget," Meier later said, "that many of our troopers were 'mean machines.' A little bit of pressure on the trigger meant the difference between a live prisoner and a corpse." But other factors contributed to the dearth of prisoners; Joe Pistone of F/502 recalls capturing a badly wounded German officer who refused a blood transfusion because it wasn't pure Aryan blood. As a result, the German bled to death. *Pangerl*

POWs in a snowy field, some 86 were killed and a few others feigned death and later managed to escape to tell the tale. Word of this massacre spread quickly throughout the Ardennes, which only ensured Allied retaliation and bolstered US resolve to achieve vengeance through victory.

More German armored spearheads broke through the lines in the Schnee Eifel, decimating two regiments of the 106th Inf. Div. To the south, elements of the Fifth Panzer Army were pushing the stubborn 28th Inf. Div. westward and driving toward Bastogne. After desperate fighting to delay the Germans at St. Vith, the 7th Armored would eventually withdraw. The Allies had definitely been caught by surprise, and the largest pitched battle of the ETO had begun.

Steve Chappuis Makes Bird Colonel

At Camp Mourmelon in late 1944, General Taylor pinned a bird on the collar of Chappuis before the general left to attend a conference back in Washington, D.C. Chappuis took command of the 502 after Col. Mike Michaelis was wounded twice and evacuated from Holland. *Chappuis*

Chapter Eleven

Bastogne Bound

At 0400hr on 18 December 1944, the 101st Airborne's troopers were nestled all snug in their beds at Camp Mourmelon, when troop leaders walked in and yelled, "Wake up and start getting ready; we're moving out!"

Don Burgett, A/506 heard a non-com yell, "Pack your seaborne rolls!." This meant only one thing—a return to combat.

In F/501's area, Sergeant McKenney was shouting, "Pack three rolls; we're moving out!"

Lieutenant Sefton at D/501 was sound asleep when Captain Snodgrass shook him and said, "Get up! We're committed; we're going-in." Sefton recalled:

> I thought it was a lousy joke and suggested a couple of things he could do. But he finally convinced me that we were alerted, and we were going somewhere. Information at the company level was hazy but we thought we were going in to exploit a breakthrough, which in view of the history of the war up to that point, seemed a very logical explanation of all the haste and urgency.

Leo Gillis, who had recently been transferred into S/Sgt. Joe Kenney's home for wayward souls, (2nd Platoon E/501), recalled the chaos and shortage of equipment:

> We heard all kinds of rumors, that the Germans had run over an entire American Army and they couldn't be stopped . . . It was a real gaffed-up affair as far as equipment was concerned. Everything had

been turned in after Holland. If you got a rifle you were lucky, if you got an entrenching tool, you were fabulously lucky. Clothing, boots, overcoats were all at a minimum.

Many recently-arrived replacements had not yet been trained and absorbed into their companies; the coming fight would quickly make veterans of all of them. Some men, like members of the 501's band, had been kept out of combat in the previous missions. They viewed this as possibly their last opportunity to fight in WWII. They asked Father Sampson for permission to join the combat troops, but he refused to give them permission. On the other hand, he didn't deny them permission. They quietly attached themselves to their former companies and went to battle. Bob Robertson, a drummer with C/501 would be seriously wounded by artillery in the Bois Jacques. Julius Schrader would be captured at Wardin.

Late-war fatalism had set in with some individuals. Sergeant Fletcher "Doc" Gainey, a buddy of Gillis' in F/501, had a certain feeling that he would be killed or maimed in the coming battle. A. J. Sokol of A/327 was enjoying his last few seconds in a warm bunk when his friend Sgt. Bennie Castleman said, "You know, Andy, I don't think I'm gonna make it." (A direct hit by a mortar shell on 10 January 1945 would blow off Gainey's leg at the hip. Castleman was killed by artillery fire on Christmas morning.)

The 101st's CO, Maj. Gen. Maxwell Taylor, was not present when the division moved out. He had

Bastogne Bound
Lieutenant Corey Shepard (I/502), Lt. Ralph Watson (G/502), and Sgt. Graham Armstrong (S-2/502; Armstrong later received a battlefield commission to second lieutenant) leaving Mourmelon, France, on 18 December 1944. *Pangerl*

returned for a conference in Washington D.C. following the Holland operation. In Taylor's absence, Brigadier General Anthony C. "Tony" McAuliffe, the division artillery commander would serve as acting division CO.

Scores of 101st troopers were visiting Paris when the alert happened, and Maj. Cecil L. Simmons was assigned to round them up and put them on a train back to Mourmelon.

Starting at midday and continuing into the evening of 18 December, units of the 101st loaded onto large open-backed semi trucks and departed Mourmelon for Belgium, a trip of over 200 miles. General McAuliffe and an advance party rode up ahead of the division. The 82nd Airborne had also been alerted to move against the German Bulge from the Reims area. They departed first, passing through the Belgian city of Bastogne and continuing northward to Werbomont. There they would dismount and head east to join the fighting at Cheneux and points south along the Ambleve River.

General Troy Middleton's VIII Corps HQ had been in Bastogne, a town where seven roads and two railroad lines converge. The town had been liberated by the US Army back in September, but was now threatened by advancing units of the Fifth Panzer Army. Being a road and rail center in the path of the German breakthrough, it was logically an important place to establish a defense. Thus, with the 82nd Airborne already gone to the north, arriving trucks bearing the 101st Airborne were diverted to fields west of Bastogne, near Mande St. Etienne and neighboring villages. The troops would jump off their trucks, crawl under the pine trees, and get a few hours of chilly sleep before moving out.

Gillis recalled the truck ride from Mourmelon:

We loaded onto these great big semis, and they were brand-new trucks. Brand-new. I remember Ed Turer—we had said goodbye to him in the hospital. We were in the trucks, we were *moving*, going down the road, and here comes Turer, running along behind us, with his hospital pajamas on, wearing boots, not laced-up. We pulled him aboard the truck. Even though he was real sick when we saw him in the hospital, he decided that he wasn't as sick as he thought he was.

The troops were forced to stand up during the 12hr drive, and after darkness, the convoy hurtled on with headlights ablaze in violation of usual blackout procedures.

The 101st Airborne and Fifth Panzer Army weren't the only military units converging on Bastogne at that moment. Elements of the 9th and 10th Armored Div., VIII Corps Artillery, and two engineer battalions also took part in the defense of Bastogne.

Stragglers from miscellaneous units who chose to stay and fight at Bastogne were organized into Team SNAFU. By 21 December, the German Wehrmacht would have Bastogne completely surrounded. The defending garrison would successfully hold out against elements of seven German divisions until 26 December, when relief forces of the Third Army would break through from the south.

The 101st Airborne provided some 11,000 of the defense troops, but an approximately equal number were provided by all the miscellaneous units also trapped there.

That night, near Margaret, east of Bastogne, Team Cherry of the US 10th Armored Div. had played a crucial role in delaying the Panzer Lehr Div. from entering Bastogne from the east. The resultant delays gave the 501 time to move east from Bastogne and meet Panzer Lehr head-on in the morning, some miles east of Bastogne. There, the intrepid paratroopers, aided by 105mm cannons of the 907 and men and vehicles of Team Cherry, were able to stop the Panzer Lehr.

As paratroopers moved out near dawn, they were sent to various towns surrounding Bastogne, small villages where the actual defensive fighting would take place. A circular defense ring was formed all around Bastogne, with the last arriving units, the 502 and the 327 positioned near the debarking area, west of Bastogne. Colonel Cooper's 463rd PFAB with 75mm howitzers had recently joined the 101st at Camp Mourmelon. The 463rd was equipped with special howitzer loads with which they had successfully knocked out German tanks and halftracks in Italy and France. Their new

colleagues were skeptical of these tales but would soon see proof that the 463rd could KO armor with their little pack howitzers.

The 506 was sent north to Noville. The 501 went east, directly in the path of the German approach. The 327 took the entire south perimeter from southeast to southwest, with the 326 in support. The 502 held the west and northwest portion of the circle, and most of the artillery units were positioned west of Bastogne.

As paratroopers, many without weapons, moved forward to meet the enemy, they passed hundreds of retreating infantrymen and scores of vehicles from tanks and halftracks, to jeeps. Some men tried to borrow a weapon from the retreating troops, without success. One paratrooper was carrying a large tree branch. He shook it aggressively in the direction of the enemy for the benefit of those going the opposite way. "By this evening I'm gonna have me a Mauser rifle," he said.

Tommy Thomas of F/501 was armed only with a nightstick he had "liberated" from an MP in Reims. He was twirling it in contempt of the oncoming German might as his unit marched toward Bizory.

Emerson Rhodes saw retreating troops race past clinging to a westbound jeep. "You'll be soooorrrrryyyyy . . . " they called.

A major in a retreating vehicle called out "You'll never stop 'em boys!"

"We're going to have a try at it, sir," replied Lyle Snyder of F/501.

Moving toward Bizory, Sgt. Joe Bass of the 501 encountered a retreating halftrack, driven by a lieutenant. Bass stopped the vehicle, pointed his M-1 at the officer and said "You can go, lieutenant, but you're leaving that vehicle here!"

Thus, Bass commandeered a halftrack which later came in handy for hauling heavy weapons and ammunition. His men would later drive it as far as Alsace.

By morning of 19 December 1944, the stage had been set for the Battle of Bastogne, one of the most dramatic battles of American military history.

Some of the troopers passed the road signs and asked: "What's a 'Bas-TOG-neee?'"

But Jim "Pee-Wee" Martin of G/506 had a premonition. "Take a good look at the name on that sign," he told his friends, "because we're gonna make history here."

Chapter Twelve

Noville and Foy

The village of Noville, Belgium, lies some 5–6 miles north of Bastogne, and on 19 December it was being held by troops of the 10th Armored Div., soldiers under the command of Major Desobry. Elements of the 2nd Panzer Div. were bypassing Noville to the north in their westward drive, but by holding the village, the road coming into Bastogne from the north was blocked. Desobry was already asking for permission to withdraw his forces from Noville. But he was told to hold it as long as possible and that a battalion of paratroopers would be sent north to reinforce him. This was the 1/506. While in Noville, the 1/506 CO would be killed by an artillery hit on his CP. Major Bob Harwick would replace LaPrade as battalion CO.

Company A led 1/506's northward march from Bastogne to Noville, and passed the smaller village of Foy en route. At the side of the road a jeep trailer had been parked, filled with bandoliers of ammunition, some grenades, and boxes of loose .45cal ball ammo. The ammunition was handed to troopers as they walked past. Many were still without a weapon. Don Burgett was handed several handfuls of loose .45cal ammo, which he stuffed into his pockets for his pistol. His former platoon sergeant, S/Sgt. Ted Vetland had just rejoined the regiment after being wounded in Holland. Vetland was among those entering Noville without a weapon. But he would later borrow Charlie Syers' bazooka and venture out in the thick fog, firing three rockets at as many German tanks. Vetland was awarded the Silver Star for crippling one of them and knocking out another.

Thick fog, formerly an asset to the Germans in their surprise offensive, had grounded Allied planes. But at Noville, it would enable the outnumbered American forces to survive in the face of massive German manpower and tanks. The lightly armed paratroopers would find themselves in the midst of this mighty force, always outnumbered and outgunned, but their invisibility in the pea soup mists protected them.

To Don Burgett, "The fog was like looking into a glass of milk." To Hank DiCarlo, who fought nearby

Kangaroo Headquarters
Divisional CP for the 101st Airborne during the Bastogne siege was in this complex of Belgian Army barracks just north of town. *Macri*

Historic Figures
Several historic figures in the Bastogne drama hold aloft one of the more pristine signs for an official photo. Left to right: Maj. Paul Danahy (G-2), Gen. Anthony McAuliffe, and Lt. Col. Harry Kinnard (G-3). *US Army*

Temporary Graves
Temporary burial of American dead in the civilian cemetery in Bastogne; they would later be reinterred at Henri Chapelle or the US Cemetery in Luxembourg. *Krochka*

at Foy, "The fog went up and down like a theater curtain."

The German tanks often emitted little engine noise, even when driving past, and sometimes the fog would lift to reveal an enemy tank only 15–20ft away from an occupied American foxhole.

As the battalion marched up toward Noville, Col. Robert Sink spotted S/Sgt. Charles A. Mitchell leading the 3rd Platoon of B/506. Sink took him aside and already knew that "Mitch" was soon to be commissioned on the battlefield to second lieutenant. Sink told him, "Sergeant Mitchell, before

Clear Skies at Last
On 23 December, one day after the German surrender ultimatum was delivered, the fog lifted enabling troop-carrier planes to make a massive resupply drop. This view across the rooftops of Bastogne was recorded by Al Krochka. *Krochka*

morning, you're gonna see more Kraut tanks than you've ever seen before. You're going to want to leave, but you're going to remember that I told you not to . . ."

With this grim forecast, Mitchell and the rest of his battalion moved up to carry out a seemingly suicidal assignment: hold Noville until authorized to withdraw, regardless of the odds.

After arriving in town, A/ and C/506 went east to occupy a ridge of high ground outside the village. After crossing a wide field, they climbed the ridge to see many German tanks facing them right on the opposite slope. The troopers faded back and dug a defensive line just east of town.

During that long, long night spent at Noville, most of the troopers continued their struggle to stay alive, whether in the cellar of a Belgian farmhouse or in a frigid foxhole.

Don Straith lay in a cemetery on the north edge of town, sweating out incoming mortar shells until he was wounded and evacuated. His ambulance was ambushed while driving south and was the last one to get out of Bastogne before the town was completely encircled. Straith's helmet was nicked by a bullet that penetrated the ambulance.

Throughout the night, German armor passed through US positions and skirted the town. The thick fog continued to hide the Americans.

"Up Yours, You Sonofabitch!"
The B/506 sector became the focus of a sharp firefight in the wee morning hours. Sergeant Mitchell had the 3rd Platoon on the right flank. His sector had been quiet and uneventful. Suddenly to his left, all hell broke loose as 1st Platoon came under attack.

Bois Jacques, Near Foy
This foxhole scene was shot by Forrest Guth of E/506. *via Winters*

Don Burgett
Private Donald R. Burgett of A/506 survived Noville and fought in the woods between Luzery and the railroad track. *Burgett*

Sergeant George Pufflet was leading 1st Platoon at the time, and Mitchell recalled that Pufflet "was crazy as a run-over dog." But 1st Platoon's radioman, Len Mackey was yelling over the radio: "Hell, they're all over us! Get some help here fast!"

Mitchell made a snap decision to move his 3rd Platoon men to the left to assist Pufflet's group. Not only had Mitchell's sector been quiet, but he reasoned that if the Germans overwhelmed 1st Platoon, they would be coming for his group next.

First Platoon was holding a tall, impressive chateau, with the usual barns and farm sheds as part of the complex. The German platoon had worked right up into the series of buildings, and the fighting was crazy and at point-blank range.

Just as Mitchell joined the 1st Platoon group in the courtyard, he heard the German platoon leader shout in English, "Handee Up!" The German officer had climbed up onto a second floor balcony, looking down on the courtyard. In the courtyard below was Hank Gogola.

In reply to the German's surrender order, Hank shouted "Up yours, you sonofabitch!" He illuminated the German officer's face momentarily with his flashlight, then fired one round from his "liberated" Luger. The bullet went into the open mouth of the enemy troop leader, and the officer toppled face first over the balcony and landed in the courtyard with a thud.

With their leader dead, the remaining Germans panicked, seeming to lose momentum in their attack. The shooting continued almost until dawn, when the German survivors withdrew, leaving behind 40 of their dead.

Sergeant Mitchell said: "We stayed there long enough to kill anything that looked like a Kraut." Mitchell had no idea where 2nd Platoon was, but B/506 would eventually join the withdrawal from Noville.

Withdrawing from Noville

When General McAuliffe finally authorized 1/506 to pull out of Noville, they had made an epic 48hr stand, denying the Germans entry on the northern approach to Bastogne. At 1315hr on 20 December, the withdrawal began, with the numerous wounded loaded onto halftracks and any available vehicles. The C/506 had just led off when Lt. Joe Reed suddenly spotted a German position as the fog lifted momentarily. He shot the Germans pointblank

Goethe and Reeves
Troopers of B/506 Ross Goethe and Bob Reeves. Goethe pulled a German into his foxhole and knifed him, throwing him back out again. *Reeves*

with his Tommygun. The fog once again proved an ally to the Americans, shielding the column until it was 500yd short of Foy.

When the lead vehicle stopped suddenly, a multiple rear end collision of armored vehicles took place, and German troops opened fire from ditches on both sides of the single, tree-lined road. The turret was blown off a tank, blocking the road, and the column skirted to the west of Foy. Some vehicles were manned by paratroopers who drove them or fired both the main batteries and the machine guns toward the enemy in Foy. Sgt. Eugene Esquible of C/506th was outstanding in firing a .50cal machine gun mounted atop one of the tanks. Company A formed the rearguard in Noville. They took all the available explosives and shells in the area and packed them into the Noville church, blowing the steeple down across the road to impede the Germans before they pulled out.

Before reaching relative safety near Luzery, 1/506 had lost 13 officers and 199 enlisted men.

The combined US forces during their stand in Noville had destroyed or badly crippled about 25 German tanks and shot-up half a regiment of enemy infantry.

There was no peace for the civilian populace in Noville after the US withdrawal. The German Army was back, and a special action reprisal unit produced photos taken the previous fall, showing vil-

lagers celebrating their liberation with American troops. A work detail was recruited to clear debris from the highway. Then eight male villagers were taken into a field near the Jacoby family house and shot dead, one by one. Among them was Father Delvaux, the village priest, who was the first man shot.

Luzery

Survivors of the Noville battle had barely arrived in the Luzery area north of Bastogne for some rest, when they were alerted to move out again. A reduced battalion (about 250) of Volksgrenadiers had worked in along the railroad line in the Bois Jacques forest and were now located in a patch of woods in the 506th sector. First Bn. was the only unit in reserve and was therefore available to root these Germans out. Marching north once again, 1/506 reached a wooded area, executed a right turn and moved in to locate and destroy the enemy force. The battalion was seriously understrength: A/506 totaled 58 men still standing from the Noville fight, and C/506 was also drastically understrength.

Don Burgett describes some of the action:

We took turns on point acting as scouts, and Siber Speer and Alvarado led off. Speer could spot anything first with his keen eyesight, but he had a bad habit of shouting, "There they are! There they are!" We had tried to tell him just to open fire and hit the ground when he spotted Germans. He did the same thing this time. We were in a line of skirmishers with C/506 on our left. Lieutenant Borelli had his platoon to the left of 2nd Platoon.

Suddenly, Speer said, "There they are!" He pointed, but beyond another German who he didn't see—they were well-camouflaged in white. This man was just 20ft in front of Speer and shot him in the mouth. Speer was dead before he hit the ground. As the German worked his bolt, Alvarado shot him with a carbine. I never had much faith in the carbine. The German drove the bolt home and shot Alvarado. The impact of the bullet knocked the carbine from Alvarado's hands. As he was going down, Alvarado yanked his knife out of the sheath on his leg and he jumped forward the two or three steps, whatever it took, and he finished killing the German with the knife. Since Speer and Alvarado were between us and the Germans, we couldn't fire, but when the Germans were both killed we went forward with the attack.

This was kind of a vicious attack. There were 58 of us and a platoon-size group from C/506. Jack Bram and Jerry Janes were firing machine guns from the hip. Bram seemed to have a big anger that he hadn't displayed earlier in the war, and he was shouting, "I'm a Jew! Come on you Nazi Bastards. I'll kill every one of you! I'm a Jew!"

Bielskis also had a .30cal tripod-mounted machine gun. He would fire, lift the weapon, move it forward, flop down, and fire again. We would leapfrog past each other as we moved forward. The attack slowed down, and I rolled down into a shallow spot with Liddel. He said, "Well, Donnie Boy, we're in it now! We're amongst 'em."

At that moment a tracer bullet which was just about spent, stuck in the tree between us. It was spewing these little sparks out. "Well it's time to leave this place," said Liddel as he took off. As he did, I thought he had kicked me. Later that night I discovered I had a bullet stuck in my hip bone. It wasn't all the way in, I was able to take it out. It was just about as spent as the tracer that had hit the tree.

The attack regained momentum. I saw one trooper rolling on the ground in hand-to-hand combat with a German. I couldn't get a clear shot at the German with my .45, but the trooper killed him. I went around to my right, came upon a young German, so close I didn't think I could miss. I fired pointblank at him, and it turned out that I did miss. He fired at me with his rifle and cut my helmet's chinstrap with the bullet. The buckle flipped-up and hit me in the eye with such an impact that I was knocked down. I thought the bullet had passed through my head. He raised up out of the hole and worked the bolt. I was lying face down, and I knew he was going to give me another shot. Some of Borelli's men were coming around our left flank. The German swung around, aimed at one of them and fired. I brought my M-1 up while he was cranking the bolt, and I shot him through the left cheek. It came out the right side and took his whole ear off. He dropped straight down in the hole; I ran the two or three steps to him. I grabbed him, threw him down on the edge of the hole, and laid my rifle across him, used him as a sandbag as I shot at two more Germans.

About that time, Dobrich to my left fired at the German running from our right to left, and the German burst into flames and fell to the ground. "Did you see that? Did you see that?" Dobrich asked. Evidently, the German had been carrying a Molotov cocktail to use on tanks.

Around then, Bielskis had fired the last bullet from his first belt of machine-gun ammo. He did something that he knew better . . . he raised up to his knees, opened the top of the machine gun and started to put a new belt in. I was to the right rear of him and a bullet struck him between the eyes. I saw the vapor come out the back of his head, through his helmet. He stayed on his knees with a real surprised look on his face for about the count of three, then all of a sudden he collapsed over the gun. He

was a very, very good friend of mine. About the time I collected myself and started to jump for the gun, another trooper slid in from the left and said "I'll take it!" He rolled Bielskis' body off it and finished loading it. I saw some Germans up ahead behind a log or an embankment and fired at them. I saw a couple of them go down; I knew one of them had probably shot Bielskis.

When we reached the railroad embankment, some of the Germans had run across to the other side. We could hear the 501 shooting at them.

A bazookaman saw a German running away down the road and instinctively fired his bazooka at him. The rocket hit behind him and after the dust and dirt and debris disappeared, he was gone. That bazooka was the biggest weapon used in this battle. Everything else was small arms, knives, pistols, rifles, and machine guns—no mortars or artillery fire.

We assembled back in a group after we realized all the Germans were dead or wounded. I was getting out of it mentally. Everything just closed in on me. After all the attacks and battles I'd been in I'd always been able to stand there with a few others guys and look around. I began to wonder, "Why me?" Why was I always one of the few survivors?

The smell—you never forget the smell . . . the burnt powder, raw iron, warm human blood, splintered bone where the leg used to be, the communications wire and limbs were down . . . I suddenly took aim at this badly wounded German in a hole; I was going to kill him. Just then, Phillips walked up. I looked at him and said, "Are you still alive?"

He says, "Yeah, I was gonna ask you the same thing."

I said "One of us should be dead by now." We both survived the war.

He says, "What are you doing?"

"I'm just gonna kill this Kraut."

He says "Naw, he's too badly shot-up. Leave him alone," and he pushed the barrel of my rifle away. Then an older German who had been shot in the leg came up from the left and surrendered to me. A paratrooper walked up from behind me and said, "Has he got a Luger?"

I said "No," so *Ka-Blam*! He shot the German. The German thought I shot him, so he started swearing at me, before he died. So there was just a lot of death in that one area, a lot of carnage, a lot of unnecessary killing. It seemed like everything just

How Was the States, General?
This cutting question as well as his absence in the glory days of the Bastogne siege would haunt General Taylor to the end. Many who survived those days could not forget the general's presence in Washington, D.C., when the German breakthrough happened. *Musura*

finally came in on both sides. The Germans were really vicious at this time, and we were too.

After this fight, 1/506 made a 180deg turn, heading back to the highway. Two more firefights erupted along the way, and Pvt. Charles D. Horn was killed. Mercifully, most the worst fighting for 1/506 at Bastogne had ended.

Foy

The hamlet of Foy, Belgium, was situated between the US front-line and German forces to the north, closer to Noville. For several weeks it was in no-man's land, being alternately occupied by each side. Some men estimate that the small town changed hands at least seven times. A number of sizable German groups were ambushed and decimated in the fields nearby, mostly by 2/506 troopers. Art DiMarzio of D/506 heard the ratio of nine German bodies for every dead American in the area.

The tiny village was the scene of some armored battles and was hit by P-47 fighter-bomber attacks several times. In all, eight houses in Foy were completely destroyed although only one villager was killed.

The distance between the railroad line and Recogne is considerable, and members of 2/506 and H/506 were spread quite thinly along this front. Lieutenant Alex Andros of H/506 felt that a German regiment could have marched through one of the gaps in the line, undetected.

The Apathetic SS Sentry

As reported elsewhere, the shelling, horrible weather conditions, and little prospect of relief had worn down the morale of both sides. Periodically bad news from home like a "Dear John" letter would arrive, causing some individuals to cease caring or to lose their will to survive. Conditions at the front line were such that such apathy was soon met with disaster. One foggy afternoon near the railroad line in Jack's Woods, Hank DiCarlo saw a sergeant from the 3/506 LMG platoon yelling at a lone sentry who stood near the woods across the tracks, wearing a long overcoat. The sentry stood as still as a statue, with his back to the tracks.

"Hey! Is that G Company?" the LMG sergeant yelled.

The sentry didn't answer or move.

"Hey is that G Company?" the sergeant repeated, growing angry, as the sentry was ignoring him.

Finally DiCarlo saw the agitated sergeant walk briskly across the tracks and grab the sentry by the arm.

"Dammit! Answer me when I ask you a question!"

Suddenly, the American sergeant pivoted and walked back across the tracks, past DiCarlo.

DiCarlo later learned that when the sergeant grabbed the sentry by the arm, the sentry had half-turned to face him, and he was wearing SS lightning flashes on his collar. The sergeant recoiled in shock and walked away. The German continued standing in his watch position. The exact reason for the indifference of this SS man to whatever happened around him will remain a matter of speculation.

Perhaps he was fed-up with the futility of Hitler's Ardennes offensive?

Jack's Woods

The section of dense pine forest that runs from west to east between Foy and Bizory was known as the "Bois Jacques," and the troopers came to call it "Jacks Woods." The railroad line that cuts through these woods on a 45deg angle was the boundary line between the 501 and the 506.

A large supply of burlap sacks had been discovered back in Bastogne, and a quantity of them reached 2/506. They were worn wrapped around boots to help prevent frozen feet. A large warehouse of flour had also been found in town. Cooks made pancakes with it, and jeeps carried these out to men in front-line positions. Some troopers had brought bottles of cognac from Mourmelon and used the liquor as pancake syrup.

Searching out foxholes in the dim light before dawn, the cooks would flip an ice-cold pancake into each hole with the announcement "Breakfast is served!"

Both sides did a lot of patrolling in the woods above Foy, and the Germans attempted to infiltrate

Meeting in Noville 15 January 1945. General Maxwell Taylor met with staff officers in Noville. *Musura*

during darkness on a number of occasions.

Ross Goethe from Nebraska was a member of B/506 and obviously of German descent. But he was among the most livid of German haters in his company. His buddies could not understand why Goethe was so hard on the enemy, but his buddy Bob Reeves was aware that Goethe never seemed to get any mail from home.

One night in suspenseful darkness, B/506 men were on line in the pine woods and could barely hear German scouts creeping quietly toward them along the forest floor.

One German, groping in the pitch blackness, felt the leading edge of Goethe's foxhole. Reaching forward with his bayonet in hand, the German swept the edged weapon from side to side. Goethe was laying back out of range of the bayonet, but he suddenly grabbed the German's wrist and yanked him into the foxhole, stabbed him several times with his own bayonet, then flung him back out, in the direction from which he had come. The troopers didn't want to fire their weapons in the dark as it would give their positions away. Bob Reeves, who was in the next foxhole remarked, "I don't think I would've had the guts to pull the German in the hole and knife him. I think I would've had to shoot him." The wounded German lay groaning outside Goethe's hole until almost dawn, when he finally died.

Chapter Thirteen

Bizory

The story of the 101st at Bizory is mostly the story of 2/501, with A Company also involved. The first phase started on 19 December, when 2/501 first moved east from Bastogne

Tank Destroyer
An M18 TD behind a house in Bizory. The M18s were new when the Bulge started, and a few were trapped inside Bastogne during the siege. This specimen supported 2/501. The 2/501 CO, Lt. Col. Sammie N. Homan, recalls chatting with a tank commander whose head and upper body were protruding out of the tank's turret. Suddenly, a flat-trajectory artillery shell hit the commander, pulverizing his upper body into a red spray that covered Homan's face. "Talk about waking-up with screaming nightmares," Homan later recalled. *via Leone*

and met advanced elements of a German division near Bizory. A line was established near the village, with E and F Companies on line in a perfect defensive position. There was as yet no snow on the ground, and when a battalion of Germans attacked on the early morning of 20 December, most of the American riflemen and machine gunners had a field of fire. All the available artillery in Bastogne was also massed on the German attack. The German tanks held back, and one was left behind, disabled. All the prior experience in combat had made the 501 a deadly killing organization and the Germans blundered into a veritable meat grinder.

The next day, snow blanketed the area, but no more major thrusts came from the same direction. During the rest of the siege, long-range sniping was done by both sides, with the usual exchange of mortar and artillery rounds.

On Christmas Eve, the Germans shelled the area with captured WP mortar shells and played music over loudspeakers, including Big Crosby's "White Christmas" and some Count Basie tunes. There were also propaganda leaflets shot over in a futile attempt to get the paratroopers to surrender. The 2/501 S-2 section was stationed in the cellar of the Goose family chateau on the north edge of the village. This sizable home was surrounded by a stone wall that enclosed the cobblestone courtyard. Louis Frey recalled that the German troops in the area formed a makeshift choir and serenaded the Americans with "Silent Night" and other classic carols like "Good King Wences . . ." The Germans were quite close at hand when singing. Then, around 0300hr came their

Christmas present—a counterattack in which the Germans set fire to the Goose chateau.

Frey and his friends escaped out the back, but in the garish light of the flames, he saw his friend, Allen Hurd dash into the courtyard, among the attacking Nazis, firing his M-1 rifle from the hip. Hurd must have seemed a demonic apparition to the Germans as they fell to his rifle fire. He had stuffed a long Nazi flag into his rear pants pocket, and it was dragging on the ground behind him like a crimson cape as he ran around the courtyard. The entire scene lent an air of unreality to the night.

501's Attack of 3 January

Battalions 2 and 3 of the 501 braved the enemy mortars and artillery, crossed the railroad tracks, and moved in a sweep of the forest north of the railroad.

Company G, supported by the LMG platoon, met heavy resistance as soon as they entered the trees on the north side. George "Scotty" Sciortino was killed there, and his buddy, Lee Parish was knocked down by a bullet that glanced off his helmet. A German was popping up and down in his hole, firing an MG08 like a jack-in-the box. The next time he jumped up, Joyce Chesney fired his M-1 from the hip and drilled the German gunner between the eyes.

The other companies of 2nd and 3rd Bn. met only sporadic small arms fire from deeper in the woods and fired at muzzle flashes, or guesstimated where the Germans were. The Germans in their path faded back several hundred yards. The troops dug in on a new line, held for several hours, then were ordered to fall back to the previous line.

Company E was the reserve company of 2/501 that day and were on the south fringe of the Bois Jacques expecting no action, when the attack of the 26th SS Panzer-Grenadier Reg. hit their positions. Actually, the grenadiers, accompanied by tanks and captured American halftracks, were passing the woods on an angle, intent on driving toward Bastogne itself. They overran two or three listening posts (LPs) positioned on the snowy open ground in front of the woods, but were forced to pivot toward the woods when a torrent of American bullets pelted them from the right flank.

The Germans drove their tanks and halftracks into one of the forest-surrounded alcoves south of the railroad and began pouring fire into the foxholes dug under the pine trees. Vehicles mounting 20mm flak cannons jockeyed back and forth, spraying the exploding rounds at the American positions. Deadly marksmen of the 501 picked off all Germans in sight. It was a blood bath for both sides.

Lieutenant Joe MacGregor, who had miraculously returned from the hospital after being shot in the head outside Veghel, took a bazooka and a couple of assistants and knocked out several German

Foxholes in the Snow
These foxholes are occupied by members of the 501. Visible in the background are sections of the Bois Jacques. The 501's new regimental photographer, Joe "Gopher" Sloan, snapped this nice photo. *via Wilbur*

armored vehicles. Sergeant McClure was awarded a Silver Star for manning the machine gun on a KO'd German half-track to use it against other German troops. He was wounded in the action and later received his Silver Star in the mail after returning home.

Among the HQ/2 501 men killed that day was Harry Artinger. He was walking back to the woods from an overrun LP when an MG42 sprayed him

Milky Fog
Troopers of E/501 strain to see toward the advancing Germans through thick fog in the Bois Jacques. *Leone*

The Ordeal of Charlie Eckman

As a member of 2/501's LMG platoon, Charlie Eckman had been with the regiment since Camp Toccoa. At 5ft 4in and less than 120lb, the 17-year-old trooper had been through Normandy and Holland and had gained a reputation as both the youngest and most-wounded trooper in the 501.

Around 4 January, Charlie received his 17th combat wound, a 9mm slug in the ankle, which drove a boot eyelet into his leg. As he lay on the ground in the Bois Jacques, awaiting treatment, a medic pulled off his boots and saw blackened flesh.

"My God, boy, your legs are gonna be cut off! You've got frozen limbs!"

Charlie hadn't removed his boots since coming to Bastogne as he knew his feet would swell up, preventing him from getting the boots back on. He had done toe-ups and prayed his feet wouldn't freeze. But now, it appeared, it was too late to save his feet.

A surgeon with the rank of major came up to examine Charlie's wound. Lying beside him on the ground was another paratrooper with a leg wound, and "his legs didn't hardly look dark yet," remembered Charlie

The major turned to Charlie: "What's wrong with you, boy?"

"Well, I'm wounded in the foot, sir," said Charlie, showing the major his blackened leg.

"Wounded in the foot? Hell! You ain't gonna have *legs*! You're next! Soon as I cut this boy's legs off . . ."

As Charlie recalled, the surgeon prepared to cut that troopers legs off, "right there on the damn ground. Honest to God, he had his medical supplies and saw . . . It just seemed so brutal to me."

The other wounded man said, "Well Doc, I've walked around on 'em for 24 years, but if I have to have 'em off . . ."

"Hold that kid there," the major said to Charlie. "You're next!"

"Major, you're not cuttin' my legs off."

"Don't you tell me what to do. I'm a major! What rank do you have?"

"Hey, I'm respectin' you as a doctor, but that's not a field rank. To me your rank ain't as much as mine. At least I'm a Bully-Bully Private."

"Get him the hell outta here! He's gonna die anyhow!" said the major.

Medics carried Charlie back to a tent hospital, where he was placed in a sheeted-off section and examined. In addition to his blackened legs, his throat was swollen with diptheria. Charlie was stripped naked, allowed to bathe in a tub of hot water, then placed in a bed with his feet suspended up in the air in loops.

"This is crazy! I can't get no circulation!"

A doctor entered and said "I'm sorry son, but your legs are going to have to come off. The gangrene is starting to set-in."

"No-no, give me a chance to warm up."

"No, boy, you don't understand," said the doctor. He took needles and ran them into Charlie's feet. "See? Nothing."

"Well . . . no. Give me a chance."

"Well what do you want to do, die?"

"Well, I believe so. I don't want my legs cut off."

As soon as the doctors left to have a meeting, Charlie got out of bed and "started to do push-ups and squats, and I rubbed and rubbed my legs. I heard 'em coming and I plunged back in that bed."

"Gosh darn, it looks like the color's a lot better than it was just 20min ago," the doctor said. But, "Boy, there's still no circulation."

"Well you just give me a couple of days, then I'll decide whether I want to die or have 'em cut off."

"Well I can guarantee you that in a couple of days you're gonna die."

Charlie kept squatting and exercising all night long.

He had to disconnect the intravenous tubes from his arms and "caught hell for this each time . . . I lied and told them the tubes were painful."

Each time the nurse came to check his thermometer, Charlie would plunge back into bed. "I didn't want 'em to see what I was doing or know what I was doing."

The next day, the doctor returned to examine him. "A miracle happened," the doctor said. "We were going to cut your left leg off above the knee and the right one below. But now we can cut off the left one clean below the knee, and the right one at the ankle."

"No-no . . ."

The next day the doctor said, "Jesus, boy, a miracle has indeed happened. It's because you're so damned young! Some of the feeling has come back and we're getting some blood out of your legs. We're gonna cut four toes off the left foot and three off the right. How's that, boy?"

"No, no. I want one more day."

Thus did Charlie Eckman retain both legs and all his toes. He would remain in the hospital a few months, missing only the Alsace campaign.

Eckman and Madden
Denver Madden (left; KIA in Holland), spars with Charlie Eckman (right), both were in the LMG platoon HQ/2 501. Eckman was wounded 17 times in WWII and nearly had both legs amputated at Bastogne because of gangrene. *Eckman*

and Pelham Noyes. Artinger was killed but Noyes feigned death to survive his 6th and 7th bullet wounds of the war.

A platoon of infantrymen had been hit on the open ground by a mortar barrage, which killed most of the men in the hole. German armor had then overrun the position. Artinger and Noyes had escaped from that position only to be gunned down just before reaching the woods. Later in the afternoon, Charlie Eckman and Henry Schwabe ran across the open ground to the wiped-out position. During the 200yd run, Eckman was grazed on the hip by a bullet and other rounds shattered the stock of his Tommygun. He jumped into the pit containing about 14 American bodies with "glazed eyes." Sorting through the bodies, Eckman and Schwabe found Harry Coffey of their company buried under a number of dead men. He was babbling and incoherent. After dusk, Eckman and Schwabe dragged the disoriented Coffey back to the woods.

When the German attack was at its zenith, Leo Gillis crawled out to one of the overrun outposts on the open ground and manned a bazooka with another trooper. They fired without result at some retreating German armor. Before returning to the woods, Gillis noticed an abandoned A-6 machine gun that the Germans had overrun, shoving the muzzle down into the muddy, snowy ground. As he was about to return to the woods, Gillis looked across the open area to a hay pile where a number of troopers had gotten hay to line their foxholes with the previous night.

He recalled:

I looked back over at that hay pile, and man there's all kinds of Germans standing around that hay pile. So I took that machine gun that was stuck down in the mud, faced it around, threw out the belt, and I fired 250 rounds without a miss! Man, I cut that haystack in half. You could hear the Germans yelling and everything else. I killed about a dozen guys there.

Evidently, these Germans had stopped to take a break, thinking they were out of view of the American line. They actually were, but Gillis's trip to the LP had put him in a different vantage point.

Carl Beck with H/501 relates more of the action:

We crossed the railroad track and went through the woods on the north side. The ground sloped gradually uphill for several hundred yards. This turned into an all-day affair. We went down trails into these real thick woods, looking for some American tanks that had gotten mouse-trapped.

A tanker with the "battle rattles" came walking up this trail. Someone asked him, "Where are you going?" He had on one of those long head protec-

Team O'Hara
Armored troops, probably of the 10th Armored Div.'s Team O'Hara, near Bizory. *via Newton*

tors with the visor in the rear. He said, "I gotta go get a new tank!" and continued back.

Our platoon leader was S/Sgt. Harry Plisevich; we were pretty much at full strength. He got us on line, we went down through these thick woods, firing as we went, then made a turning movement. The woods were so thick, it was hard to contact each other. I set the A-6 machine gun up on a tree that had been blown over and was able to get it up a little higher. This put us on the flank of a Volksgrenadier outfit that was moving up to relieve the SS troops in the area. They had a little tank and a big tank. The little tank was zig-zagging in front of the big tank, with the infantry following.

The infantry had their communications people unreeling wire as they moved along. The big tank shot and killed John O. Bay, and our medic Goolsby got the Silver Star for waving his red cross brassard and going out to get his body. I had the A-6 over the roots of this tree, with Duffy down beside me as second gunner.

Apparently they were going to try to flank us, because they sent a squad with an MG42 round and they were walking right toward us.

Gloom in the Bois Jacques
The gloomy atmosphere of these bitter woods northeast of Bastogne was captured in this photo of Maurice Sandquist (HQ/2 501) by Louis Frey. *Frey*

In the meantime, all these Germans are walking past saying, "Cease fire. Cease fire. "Their voices sounded like crickets, you know, under a lot of strain.

Plisevich said, "O.K., let 'em have it!" and we wasted the MG crew.

I could see the shadow of faint light coming off the helmet of the first man coming toward me with the MG42. I saw my tracer go through him, and I shot the whole squad behind him.

We had a replacement named Gussie Hill, known as "Cussless Gus" because he didn't swear. He would say, "Oh phooey!" or "Gosh darn it!" He sat on the edge of a foxhole and shot about 21 Krauts before he was hit. He shot a German major that was standing up on a mound of earth, shouting orders to his troops.

Medic Goolsby came to treat Cussless Gus and was patching up wounds to his front, when he turned Gus over and found much worse wounds on his back. Gussie died there. We lost a lot of people, but we wiped out the German unit.

A general withdrawal of 2nd and 3rd battalion troops was ordered late in the afternoon, and the Americans moved south, re-crossing the railroad track to their line of departure. The 2/501 troops could hear Germans digging in across the embankment; they had followed the US troops right back to the tracks.

Sergeant Harry Plisevich stayed on the north side of the track to help organize the withdrawal and to make sure nobody got left behind. In a large bomb crater he found a number of wounded troopers, including an I/501 man whose diaphragm seemed to have collapsed from the concussion of a near explosion. As Harry was moving through the woods, he made a wrong turn and came face to face with a German tank. He was captured and taken to the rear for interrogation in a Belgian farmhouse. While there, he saw Lt. Joseph Forney of G/501, who had also been captured that day.

Harry was to spend the duration as a POW. He weighed only 75lb when liberated. He was not a co-operative prisoner.

A Buddy's Act of Devotion

That night after darkness fell, Harry Plisevich's best buddy, Leonard Morris, was wondering why Harry hadn't returned. Was he dead, wounded, or a prisoner? Leonard couldn't stand the mystery, so he crept across the railroad embankment alone, moving quietly through the German line to prowl around for hours in the dark, enemy-held woods in search of his friend. Anyone who has visited the area can realize what an incredible act of bravery and devotion this was. Before daylight, Morris realized his search would be fruitless, and he re-crossed the railroad to US lines.

It is very easy to get lost in the Bois Jacques, and Frank Whiting of A/501 spent three lonely days wandering in these woods after A's first battle, dodging enemy patrols until he found other Americans.

By beating back the SS attack, 2/501 ended one of the most-remembered engagements they fought in WWII.

Because of the see-saw tactics of the Bois Jacques fighting, 2/501 was forced to attack sideways through the same area again on 10 January. Support on the right flank was from the 6th Armored Div. Encountering a complex of German dugouts, the F/501 men used leap-frog tactics to blast and grenade the Germans out of their holes.

The area above Bizory in the Bois Jacques figured prominently in the fighting for the next week as the 327 and the 502 pushed along the railroad line though the woods in their approach to Bourcy. (See chapter 18.)

Chapter Fourteen

Mont, Neffe, and Wardin

The towns of Mont and Neffe lie very close to each other directly east of the city of Bastogne. A squad of engineers delayed an attack by German armor on the morning of 19 December. Then on 21 December, Pvt. John Mishler of B/501 blocked another attack by knocking out the leading German tank with his bazooka, effectively blocking the road west for a critical amount of time. Mishler was seriously wounded during this act but survived to wear his Silver Star.

Battalions 2 and 3 of the 501, supported by the 907th artillery, dug-in facing east near Mont. To their right were glider troops. Despite the first contact being made at Neffe, 2/501 would repulse the first major German attempt to enter Bastogne from the east at Bizory. (See Chapter 13.)

One company of 3/501 did not settle in at Mont on 19 December. Company I had entered the fray with Lt. Claude Wallace at the helm. All the senior non-coms in the company had been transferred during the stay in Mourmelon due to a scandal started by a French camp follower.

Debacle at Wardin

Carl Sargis from B/501 replaced the erstwhile first sergeant, and S/Sgt. Erminio Calderan, formerly of D/501, had also arrived recently. These were good men, as were some of the new replacement officers. But they didn't know the individuals in I/501 nor their capabilities. The company was about to be subjected to the severest of tests, a desperate fight for survival against overwhelming German panzer forces and Tiger Royal tanks.

Colonel Julian Ewell, in retrospect, regretted the shifting of leaders in the company, but that was with hindsight. The entire Bastogne battle happened with no advance notice, and the debacle at Wardin could not have been foreseen.

The approach march to Wardin, which is over 5 miles southeast of Bastogne, took several hours. The company took a difficult route decided on by the new leaders, passing through numerous wooded areas. There was not yet snow on the ground, and many troopers shed their overcoats and other winter accessories on the sweaty, difficult approach march. They entered Wardin without resistance after turning left at a small bridge that crosses a stream on the edge of the village.

A company CP was established in a farmhouse on the north side of the street. Bill McMahon led his machine-gun section up a small rise facing south at the south edge of town. Radioman Frank Guzy had a radio but was unable to make contact with 3/501 or a group of friendly tanks that sat back to the southwest on higher ground.

Guzy later realized he was under German observation as he sought higher ground just outside Wardin on which to set up his radio. When German tanks opened fire, they started toward the church from the south. The opening 88mm round went through the CP into the attached barn, killing 1st Sgt. Carl Sargis. McMahon's group swept a line of German panzer-grenadiers coming over the ridge, then saw the tanks.

Being a survivor of Normandy and Holland, McMahon made a snap decision to get out of town

KIA in Wardin?
Captain Claude Wallace, CO of I/501, was KIA on 19 December 1944, the day the company entered Wardin, Belgium. According to most accounts, Wallace died near Lieutenant Shoemaker in Wardin, but some survivors of the company claim he actually died several days later.
Hamilton

as quickly as possible. He told his squad to take off, heading north. They re-crossed the main road in town, leaving the LMG behind with much other equipment. Given cover by smoke from the exploding tanks shells, the retreating troopers splashed right through the stream on the far edge of town and made their way uphill to the nearest patch of woods. From there, they watched the town burn.

Marvin Wolfe witnessed a crucial action by Wilbrod Gauthier of his company. Gauthier was normally a machine-gunner. After firing an LMG for awhile, Gauthier left the gun and ran onto the road with a bazooka. He fired a rocket into the lead tank, disabling it and causing a critical delay for the Germans. This enabled many of his comrades to escape from the town. Gauthier was killed by machine-gun fire from another tank in the process. He remains one of the many heroes who was never decorated for his heroism.

Of the 140 men who went into Wardin on the 19th, only 83 escaped to reorganize the following day. The survivors made their way back piecemeal, surviving any way they could.

Erminio Calderan and Robert Vaughn joined a group of Belgian civilians who were walking west, pushing their possessions along in carts. The troopers obtained a woman's coat and dress and donned them, then walked west in the group, pushing a baby carriage. The Germans in the distance spotted their boots and opened fire. The duo hit the ditch and managed to make their escape.

Richard Hahlbohm survived Wardin but was taken prisoner. Hahlbohm wrote of his experience:

Wardin is a small town, about 6 or 7 houses, and was of no value to us or the enemy. We were just to find out where the enemy were. Believe me—we did.

There was a long wood pile, neatly stacked to my side, so I crouched behind it. I was waiting for the Krauts to come through the hedgerow, but they must have backed-off. I then heard a tank coming up the road. He stopped in plain sight of me, to my left. I noticed right away it was a new Tiger Royal. He was firing down into the open field.

I gathered that my company, or a part of it

was making a run for it as we only had bazookas to fire at them. The tank's machine gunner was firing, but he didn't see me. I looked over my shoulder and saw my buddy Julius J. Schrader behind a tree to my left. I was in the only position to fire at the tank. I noticed behind the corner of the house was a bazookaman. I yelled, "Tank!" and pointed. When I took another look, the bazooka was there, but the gunner wasn't.

Meanwhile, I had knocked off the machine-gunner in the tank turret and drew attention. The 88 swung in my direction. I knew he couldn't penetrate the whole wood pile with his first shot so I got up on my haunches to make a dash behind the house after he let the first one fly. But he realized this also, so he backed his gun up to make a ricochet shot from the house so it would get me and whoever was in back of the house.

I figured now was the time to make tracks, as a new turret gunner was peppering the area. I started my 10–12ft leap, and he let loose and the bullets imbedded in the house. The 88 concussion caught me halfways there. It made me like a rag doll flying through the air. As I hit the ground, I heard the machine gun open up at the same time. Someone pulled me behind the house. My overcoat was ripped in a few places by shrapnel, but luckily, I wasn't hit.

We took refuge in the house. My ears were ringing like two dozen phones. We were trapped in the house. As we were preparing to fight from the house, it caught on fire. As I looked out the window I saw wall-to-wall Krauts. It looked like a whole regiment. After a few minutes of debate I told the other seven men with me to break down their weapons and scatter them all over and in the walls as I had heard the Krauts shot you with your own weapons. Surrender was a bitter pill to swallow, but we had to survive. I was wondering how Captain Wallace, my CO, was making out and hoped he saw the odds against him.

They took us out and put us up against a hedgerow and brought up a GI halftrack with a .50cal on top. The gunner cranked in a round and leveled the gun on us. I figured we had had it for sure. A machine gunner who had been wounded earlier was shot through the ass, in and out. His bandage was falling off. I forgot about being a prisoner and leaned over to push the bandage back on. I almost got shot for my trouble. So I quickly said in German, "My comrade has been wounded."

The Germans took one look at his wound and all started to laugh. The interrogation officer came

Battered Bastards
Ballard's Battered Bastards of the Battling Bastion of Bastogne, Belgium. These HQ/501 survivors proudly display a bullet-riddled sign. Standing, left to right: Waldo Brown, Jim Ganter, Belgian civilian, R. J. Wilbur, Dave Smith, Chief Sayers, Joe Sloan (photographer), and Budd. Front, left to right: Eugene Amburgey, W. C. Dunn, Ted Becker, Bill Canfield (holding sign), and Duane Henson. *Sloan*

out and took us away. They put us against the hedgerow two more times and again we were saved by the officer. He then took us to the rear.

The survivors of I/501 regrouped at the regimental CP in the Bastogne seminary or at the farmhouse CP of 3/501 at Mont. They were used to fill-in on the lines.

Around 2000hr on the night of 20 December, the Germans began a concerted effort to break through the 501's lines in the Neffe-Mont area. Enemy troops moved along the highway toward 1/501, supported by several tanks. Another concentration of Germans stormed 3/501 along a slope between Neffe-Mont. This group also had tank support, but in both sectors, the German armor held back, never becoming a serious threat. A series of barbed-wire fences and cattle pens covered the area in front of 3/501, and the advancing enemy had to pause to climb each fence. Cross-firing US machine guns tore them to ribbons.

Team O'Hara

Farther south, Lt. Bill Russo with his C/501 platoon was dug-in next to Lt. John Sallin with his B/501 platoon. The brunt of the attack in that sector was taken by 10th Armored tanks from Team O'Hara. Asked Russo:

Have you ever heard of Team O'Hara? Well, they should get more credit because they really took the brunt of that attack. We could hear tank guns firing, and we didn't have any. They really

Work Detail
Prisoners on work detail, clearing rubble and debris from roads inside Bastogne. Their guard is identified as a member of HQ/326 by his helmet stencil. *Tocco*

got a whacking, buddy.

One thing I used to do, and Sallin on my right knew about it: take a German machine gun with white tracers, and fire it at them when they attack. You want to cause some confusion . . . all the way back to Berchtesgaden . . . They'll back off every time! They have to! Because who is it firing at them? When you're moving around like that things happen. Sometimes your own troops fire at you.

Whatever the Germans do, they'll do twice. You know, your men are kind of slack after a little shoot-out? I used to tell all of my gunners: "Reload and loosen all your belts because they're gonna be back" And Goddammit they were within 10min. They'll do it twice. I don't know if it was a matter that they couldn't go back and say they failed, I don't know. But it was ridiculous. I couldn't understand the Germans making their troops walk over their dead to get to us.

That's not too damn encouraging. You know, their dead still laying there?

Mayor of Bastogne
During the battle, Mr. Leon Jacquemin was mayor of Bastogne (center); he is shown here behind an American ambulance, with other city officials. *Musura*

Wounded Monument
A WWI statue in Bastogne. The WWI monument was situated near the center of town until a direct hit by a German bomb or artillery shell blew it to pieces. *Krochka*

They were so desperate. That army was shot, I'm telling you.

Among the LMG crews of 3/501 that night was Carl Beck with assistant Dick Duffy and their LMG. Beck has described his part in the repulse of the enemy attack:

We occupied a position along a sunken road where this M18 tank destroyer [TD] was in turret defilade. A machine-gun section from HQ/3 got knocked out near the haystack. The Germans were attacking at night, and it was so foggy that when a flare went up all you would see was a glow; you couldn't distinguish anything except movement. The haystack had been set afire by tracers, and Captain Hilton asked me to go out up this cut bank next to that TD and shove my machine gun through that fence line and set up final protective fires.

We were able to do that, although we were taking intense small arms fire. We started firing and fired for 15–20min out there.

The TD near me could swing his turret around and fire the .50cal machine gun from the turret. As I was moving up, they fired the 76mm main battery, which knocked me down. A .31cal bullet went bouncing off the bipod, which further complicated matters. The TD guy kept on firing the .50cal. We continued firing until the enemy was on the run; of course we couldn't see them, but their firing slowed.

They left me a little souvenir with a potato masher grenade, which exploded right off the end

In 1989, the author located the same (repaired) monument in front of the seminary where the 501's CP had been. Damage is still evident, despite repairs, and half the wounded man's head lies on the base of the monument now.

of the machine gun and threw a bunch of shrapnel in my head and face. It was dark and all I could feel was a lot of blood. Duffy remarked, "He's bleeding like a stuck hog."

They carried me down the bank past this M18, and a medic took me down the road to an aid station set up in this house, where I was treated and patched up. There were no evacuation procedures because there was no place to go. The Krauts had overrun our hospital.

While we were in this aid station, another M18 came around the corner and fired his main battery, I don't know at what. This huge piece of furniture came over and landed on all of us that were lying rolled up on stretchers. That helped relieve the tension a little bit. Well somebody set this furniture back up and got it off of us.

A few minutes later, here came that gunner who had been firing that .50cal off the turret of that M18, and he had a .31cal bullet lodged up in his nose. He come shakin' in there sayin', "Hey! You know I saw those damn things comin' but I couldn't duck in time!" What had happened was somebody fired a machine gun at him, and one of the rounds hit the ring mount, ricocheted down, and hit him in the nose. But he was all right; he was still cussin' the next morning.

Anyways, the people I knew had nowhere to go, so we just went back to the outfit. We were so low on ammunition that another attack might've finished us off. By the way, there was 72 dead out there the next morning when we got back on the line. Apparently that took a lot of starch out of 'em because we weren't hit again on that part of the line, except by some artillery.

New Year's Eve at Neffe

It was New Years Eve, and 1st Platoon of F/501 had been moved down to the Neffe sector. They had ringside seats to observe an attack by the 6th Armored Div. to take the town.

Tanks approached through the cover of the woods, crossed the railroad track, and started across an open field toward the small town. Neffe erupted with small arms and Panzerfaust fire. The attack of the tanks stalled and numerous armored infantrymen lay bleeding in the snow.

Sergeant Joe Bass of F/501 was observing, got frustrated and said, "They're gonna *die* out there!"

When he could stand it no longer, Bass recruited a team of troopers, and the 12-man group swung through the woods as the tanks had done. A "Mexican Standoff" had developed. The Germans had retreated to the cellars with their Panzer-fausts and were afraid to come out. The tankers were unwilling to go in and get them.

Bass led his group past the tanks, saw the infantry lying in the snow, and in Sgt. Charlie Palmer's words, "Made a beeline straight into Neffe." Bass entered the first house with two of his men, burst into the cellar and shouted "Hande Hoch! Komm sie raus! Schnell!"

A small group of Germans came out to surrender.

Gradually, the remaining Germans peeked out, saw that their comrades were not being shot, and a general surrender began. "It was just a case of being brave enough to go in and get them," said Palmer.

The armored officer in charge asked "Where do you get these men?" The armor then drove the rest of the way through town to consolidate the newly gained territory.

Sergeant Tom Enright had the opportunity to observe a ten man group of German prisoners taken in Neffe that afternoon. The prisoners stood shoulder to shoulder and, remembered Enright:

I suppose most of them were in their early twenties, and good-looking soldiers: well-dressed, neat, their hair was cut. You kinda had to admire them as being soldiers. But they're all standing there at Heil Hitler attention, and one of 'em on the end could speak English. But he was telling us that they were going to go to Antwerp, then sail to Canada and invade the United States. I'm sure that they believed this . . . He'd say this and the rest would answer "Ja-Ja, Ja-Ja." I'm sure they understood what he was saying, because they knew when to say "Ja-Ja" . . . My God, it was like a puppet show or something. Not really, but whatever this guy on the end said, the others chimed-in.

"Just what would you bastards say if I told you I'm gonna shoot the whole lot of you right now?," asked Sergeant Bass.

"We aren't afraid of that," said the guy on the end, "because our comrades would find our bodies and then they will kill all of you!"

"Ja-Ja, Ja-Ja," said the chorus.

Tragedy at the Seminary

Although the seminary in Bastogne wasn't actually in any of the chapter towns, it was not far from Mont on the east edge of the city. On 5 January, a tragedy occurred in the courtyard of the seminary. The building had served as a field hospital and regimental HQ for the 501.

On 5 January, a detail of men from the 501's demolitions platoon was loading a truck with land mines. Leo Runge was in the vicinity and noticed that some of the safety pins were missing from the mines. He pointed this out to the men on the loading detail, but they didn't seem too concerned.

When a considerable number of mines had been loaded, the truck suddenly exploded, instantly vaporizing some eleven to fourteen men. The exact number will never be known, but a list of eleven names is known for certain: Pvt. Frank Baer, Pvt. Walter Craley, Pvt. Michael Balducci, Pvt. Walter Dieffenbach, Pvt. Harold Brisco, Pvt. James A. Keel, S/Sgt. Leon W. Brown, Pfc. Sam P. Lapin, Cpl. Bonnie Caroon, Pvt. Elmer A. Newmann, and Pvt. Latcher Coney.

A crude small marker was erected there immediately after WWII, but medic Richard E. O'Brien visited the spot over 40 years later and discovered the sign was missing. Through his tireless efforts, a new marker has recently been placed at the spot, in tribute to the men who died there.

A number of artillery shells hit the roof of the seminary during the siege, and the stained glass rained down on the wounded men inside. Another unforgettable incident happened when a 500lb bomb came through the roof during a German air raid, went through the floor into the basement and failed to explode.

A Tragic Accident
A view of the truck that exploded in the seminary courtyard near the 501's CP in Bastogne on 5 January 1945. Along with the truck, over a dozen members of the demolitions platoon were vaporized in the terrific blast. *Duggins*

Chapter Fifteen

Marvie

A small village on the southeast corner of the Bastogne perimeter, Marvie became a focal point of several German attacks, as it was situated near a road that enters the city of Bastogne. Lieutenant Colonel Inman's 2/327 glider infantry

Sergeant Carl Dickinson of F/327 met the German ultimatum party on the Arlon road on 22 December. Carl missed out on much of the subsequent publicity, as he was wounded and evacuated in January 1945. *Dickinson*

were joined there in the defense by C/326 engineers, a platoon each from B/326 and A/501, several half-tracks and tanks of 10th Armored's Team O'Hara, and anchored on the flank by elements of 1/501. (See Chapter 14.)

On 20 December, the first German attack came in, a brisk charge by four German tanks and six half-tracks, accompanied by infantry. Two of the German tanks were KO'd by side shots from American tanks, another was hit by bazooka fire, and the last one retreated. A self-propelled gun was hit and burned as infantry infiltrated houses in the village, where fighting continued.

At 1840hr on 23 December, the Germans launched another attack, surrounding a platoon of G/327 on Hill 500, south of Marvie. Also on that hill were members of C/326. Some of these troops managed to retreat to Marvie, but others were killed or taken prisoner.

An American halftrack met the German attack head-on and retreated north into Marvie at top speed. This vehicle was mistakenly knocked out by friendly fire, but later served as an effective road-block in preventing the German armor that followed from passing through Marvie. Two German tanks were halted there, and a self-propelled gun was hit by an American tank and burst into flames in the fading light. Tanks and infantry of Team O'Hara pulled back 100yd to the west.

Returning to the night fighting in Marvie, the German infantrymen were silhouetted by flames from burning houses in the village, which aided the troopers in shooting them. Yet another German tank found the narrow road blocked by the knocked out halftrack and was blown up while turning to go back.

A failed daytime attack in the nearby F/327 sector was repulsed by men of Lieutenant Smith's platoon and acting platoon leader S/Sgt. Oswald Butler. A truce was called, allowing the Germans to pickup their wounded.

Demand for Surrender

To the right of Marvie as the perimeter faced south, is the highway running from Bastogne to Remoi-Fosse. F/327 had a defense line dug-in perpendicular to the road, with E/327 on their left. Two significant night attacks had hit this section of the perimeter, with one of them overrunning part of E/327.

It was along this road that a group of German "parliamentaries" came on the afternoon of 22 December. Leo Palma, a Browning Automatic Rifle (BAR) man, and his assistant gunner were in a foxhole in the ditch beside the road. But S/Sgt. Carl Dickinson went forward to meet the German group.

Dickinson recalled three enlisted men walking in front, the center man waving a large white flag, the men on either side waving smaller ones. Following closely behind them were two German officers with shiny jackboots and leather overcoats. The infantry major could only speak German. The medical captain spoke fluent English.

The captain announced himself to Dickinson, stating, "According to the Hague and Geneva Conferences, we have the right to parley."

Word spread quickly along the line that there was a cease-fire, and the troops got up to stretch, shave, and write letters home; they assumed that the Germans were trying to surrender to them. But it was quite the opposite. The Germans came bearing a written ultimatum, presumably authored by General von Luttwitz, which threatened total annihilation of Bastogne and its defenders if the US forces didn't surrender within 2hr.

Leo Premetz, an F/327 medic who could speak German was summoned from the platoon CP in a nearby house, but with the English-speaking German captain, translations weren't necessary. The three German enlisted men were left at Palma's foxhole. The two officers were blindfolded and led to the company CP, where they were held while their written surrender demand was carried back to HQ/101 in Bastogne.

General McAuliffe was handed the message but was preoccupied with other matters. He crumpled the letter and said, "Nuts." Upon learning that the Germans were awaiting a formal written response, he was at a loss as to what he should write. Harry Kinnard told him, "Your first remark would be hard to beat."

"What did I say?" McAuliffe asked.

Safe Snow
Sergeant Howard J. Sloan gets safe snow for coffee on 10 January 1945. *Signal Corps*

"You said 'Nuts,'" Kinnard reminded him.
A formal note was typed:

To the German Commander:
NUTS
The American Commander.

Colonel Harper, commanding the 327, was delighted with the response, and elected to deliver it personally to the German emissaries. He traveled back to the F/327 area by jeep. The German officers were led back to the foxhole line, still blindfolded.

Herding POWs
Surrendering Germans being herded toward Bastogne. *Mihok*

On the Move
Left to right: Pfc. M. L. Dickman, Pvt. Sunny Sundquist, and Sgt. Francis McCann. Dickman and McCann were members of F/327. How Sundquist (H/506) wound up with them in this photo on 30 December 1944 is a mystery Sunny's H/506 buddies are still pondering. *US Army*

The German medical officer said, "I'd rather be walking in the park with my wife."

The Germans were unblindfolded and handed the note with General McAuliffe's reply.

They were puzzled as to the meaning of "Nuts."

"It means go take a flying shit at yourself," Harper explained.

The Germans were still confused.

Harper lost his temper and said, "Nuts is strictly negative; it means the same thing as 'Go to Hell!' If you continue this foolish attack, we will kill every goddam German who tries to break into Bastogne!"

The Germans stood stiffly to attention.

"We will kill many Americans; this is war."

"On your way, bud, and good luck to you," said Harper, later regretting he had wished them luck.

The exact text of the surrender ultimatum was reproduced in McAuliffe's famous Christmas Message to the troops.

Word of the surrender ultimatum soon reached all parts of the defense perimeter, and the troops braced themselves for an anticipated avalanche of 240mm artillery shells. Curiously, the sector where the ultimatum had been delivered was not hit until two days later. But some parts of the perimeter did get an unspectacular barrage that afternoon. The later barrage hit F/327 heavily and succeeded in killing two forward observers from an artillery outfit.

As of 1800hr on 24 December , Colonel Harper's 327 was given responsibility for the perimeter from Marvie to northwest of Hemroulle—over half the total circle around Bastogne. Due to heavy forestation to the south of the city, that area was considered less suitable for passage by German tanks.

On 26 December in the same sector, the first tanks of Creighton Abrams' 4th Armored Div., Third Army, made contact with Lt. Duane J. Webster of the 326, and the encirclement of Bastogne was officially ended.

Far from being the end of the ordeal of the 101st in the Battle of the Bulge, it was just the beginning.

Chapter Sixteen

The West Perimeter— Hemroulle, Savy, Champs, Rolle

On 19 December, the 463rd PFAB arrived near the gently rolling hills at Hemroulle. On arrival, Hank Rodenbach yelled, "Hey Colonel, we can't dig-in here . . . there's no trees for the officers to hide behind!"

The 463 set up their positions there, facing west, and not far away, the 377 set up their 75mm gun positions near the village of Savy.

Although the west side of Bastogne was skirted by both the 2nd and 116th panzer divisions, their concern was mainly to bypass Bastogne and continue westward toward their objective—the Meuse River.

When the first concerted attacks came from the west after 23 December, the artillery units played a significant role in repulsing them.

The area west and especially far west of Bastogne, was initially considered to be in the rear and thus safe from German attack. Thus, the 326th Medical Company and hospital were set up near the Bois de Chabry, at crossroads X, so named because the road running southwest from Bertogne forms a perfect X with the road running west out of Bastogne.

On the night of 19–20 December, the hospital was overrun, and most of its staff and patients were captured or killed by a German armored unit. This was long believed to be group from the 2nd Panzer Div., but extensive research by Belgian historian Andre Meurisse indicates it was more likely an element of the 116th Panzer Div.

While attempting to retrieve medical supplies from the captured hospital, Father Francis Sampson, Catholic chaplain of the 501 was captured and spent the duration as a POW.

Elsewhere on the west perimeter, Captain Swanson's A/502 was initially deployed to the right flank near Monaville, but would be rotated to the west. They were in position near Champs on Christmas Eve to repulse a concerted German attack from the west.

Chateau Rolle

A medieval chateau owned by the Rolle family and still inhabited by Madame Rolle and her infant son became the CP of Col. Steve Chappuis' regiment. In the barns and surrounding buildings, members of HQ/502 and service companies made improvised billets. A number of S-2 patrols were launched from here to determine enemy strength and intentions to the north and west. Lieutenant David White had recently joined the 502 and now commanded the S-2 section. He personally accompanied most of the S-2 patrols, one of which went as far as a wooded ridge overlooking Gives.

From concealment on the ridge, patrol members could see numerous American vehicles moving in the distance. It was believed but not confirmed that these were captured vehicles, currently being driven by German troops. Many rumors had circulated of German troops speaking English wearing captured US uniforms and infiltrating the lines. Everyone was paranoid of this, and the S-2 patrol had encountered a "questionable" M-8 armored car while moving toward Gives. The commander had blond hair and a large handlebar mustache. The S-2 scouts were about to blast him, but decided not to when he shouted, "Christ! Don't shoot!"

Captain Frank Lillyman, of Normandy pathfinders fame, served in HQ/3 502 at Bastogne. *White*

Legendary Leader
Captain Wally Swanson, legendary leader of A/502, whose men repulsed the German attack on Champs on Christmas morning. Wally is shown in partial snow camouflage.

Coming back toward Ruette, the S-2 men hitched a ride with a column from the 705th Tank Destroyer Bn.'s recon utfit. The column consisted of three M-8 armored cars and two or three jeeps. Dick Ladd rode facing backward on the last M-8. Behind the M-8 was a jeep with a .30cal LMG mounted on it. When Ladd's M-8 took a turn behind a building, a Volkswagen loaded with four or five Germans fell in behind the M-8. Ladd realized the safety was "on" on his Tommygun. In the seconds it took to re-lease the safety, a German in the VW cut loose with an MP40. The slugs ripped into both of Ladd's hands and splintered the wood stock of the Tommy-gun, spraying pieces of wood in his face.

Meanwhile, the following American jeep round-ed the corner, opened-up on the VW with the .30cal LMG, and caused it to crash at the side of the road. Several Germans leaped out of the vehicle and ran. Ladd wound up in an aid station west of Bastogne.

As elsewhere in the perimeter, the icy winds whipped across the area, making conditions almost unbearable for the combatants, especially those con-fined to foxholes. John Schwartz of the 502 was wearing no less than four pairs of trousers and was still cold.

Action at Flamierge

One of the first concerted German efforts to break into Bastogne from the west fell against the lines of the 401 glider infantry, also known as 3/327. Robert D. Lott of C/401 described his role in repuls-ing this powerful enemy thrust:

On the 23rd of December 1944 at an outpost of the roadblock set up near Flamierge, Belgium, I awoke that morning to find it was so cold that my M-1 Garand rifle had frozen shut since I last pulled my turn at guard during the night. The ejector was frozen shut, so I urinated on the metal parts, which was a sure way of thawing the rifle so it would be ready to use when needed.

Later that morning I left my foxhole to go into a farmhouse that was situated right behind our hole. There I stripped my rifle down, including the trig-ger group and cleaned and oiled all the parts and reassembled the weapon. I cocked it to make sure I had assembled the gun properly. Then, all hell broke loose.

I jumped up and ran out to my foxhole and noticed a group of tanks across the open field. I thought General Patton had broken through; then I noticed the type of tanks and knew we were in trouble. The tank crews and infantry following the tanks didn't seem to spot our outpost. With me at the outpost was Sgt. Robert Bowen with a Thompson SMG, our BAR man Horkay, and Jack Gresh and myself equipped with M-1 rifles. Automatic weapons were not desirable for this situation, so our M-1s would work out best against the white-clad Jerry infantry. We could now see 12 tanks and never did estimate the number on foot. For awhile, Jack and I used our M-1s to the best of our ability and tried to put as many of their troops out of commission as possible, without giving away our position and also conserving our ammunition.

For this one battle, I was given a citation for killing 22 of the enemy. I don't know who did the counting, but Jack Gresh should have credit for his share.

As we were picking off the enemy, I spotted near my hole an abandoned bazooka and one shell that was half buried in the ground. I dug the shell out, straightened the fins, and wired it up to the bazooka, taking a guess at the range. I set the sights at 350yd, hoping to hit in the general area of the tanks, if the shell ever left the tube of the bazooka. I knew the bazooka would draw fire from the tanks and give away our position, but I knew the tanks didn't like to cope with bazooka fire. It was possible this shot could delay their attack and allow us to get back to our company or get some help.

When I fired the bazooka, the shell lobbed through the air and looked like a sure miss. But to our surprise, the shell hit a Mark IV tank in its rear bogey wheel, crippled the tank, and wounded or killed a soldier walking behind it.

The tank tried to get out of the way, but would only go into a circle. All hell broke loose again! They spotted where the bazooka shell came from, and they fired everything they had. The four of us kept down, and it felt like the end of the world had come. It would take a few minutes for the smoke to clear up, so I said, "Let's get out of here." But Sgt. Bowen thought we would get help now.

The Bed Sheets of Hemroulle
The most famous story of Hemroulle involved Lt. Col. "Long John" Hanlon, CO of 1/502. He visited the mayor of Hemroulle and directed that the church bell be rung to summon the civilian inhabitants, most of whom were hiding in their cellars.

The civilians were reluctant to come out, but a message was relayed to them that the Americans lacked white snow camouflage, a situation that gave the German attackers an advantage. The villagers were asked to donate all their white bed sheets, tablecloths, and—for helmet covers—pillow cases, which they did. Hanlon promised to replace these items at some later date.

Shortly after the war, Hanlon was able to publicize this incident in the media and received hundreds of bed sheets from donors throughout the US. He returned to Hemroulle a few years later, and the mayor again tolled the church bell. This time, the populace assembled at the church and received repayment in the form of new linens, as Hanlon had promised.

Bed Sheets of Hemroulle
Promising they would eventually be replaced, Lt. Col. "Long John" Hanlon asked the villagers of Hemroulle to donate their bed sheets and pillow cases for use by his 1/502 troopers as makeshift snow camouflage. After the war ended, Hanlon made good on his promise, returning to Belgium with enough new linen for the whole village. *Benecke*

Lonely Outpost
This position was situated in front of the castle housing HQ/502 at Rolle. The .50cal machine gun is manned by a member of the Deuce. *Krochka*

When the smoke cleared, we could see the disabled tank's personnel trying to leave their tank into another tank that came up alongside it. Then the tanks withdrew over the ridge with what I assumed was the tank commander sitting up on the tank turret, waving his arms as though he was directing the other tanks. I shot my M-1 at the possible tank commander and missed him with six shots.

I thought, *My God! I had been shooting like a beginner, wasting valuable ammo and not giving the tank a lead.* Then, I aimed my seventh shot with a lead on the moving tank, and when I squeezed the trigger, I saw him reel over backwards. I then thought, *That was worth seven shots.*

In a short time, our planes came out for the first time since we had been in Bastogne defense. They flew over the battle area and never spotted the large force in the open field as the enemy. We had hoped they would finish the battle for us.

We held there until dark without much opposition. Finally, Sergeant Bowen said he would go back to get us some help and ammunition. In a couple of minutes, he came running back and said we were cut off from our troops. The Germans had circled around in back of us and were out in front of the farmhouse. We jumped up, leaving behind a can of homemade chicken soup that I had received in an early Xmas package from my aunt in Messhopen, Pennsylvania. We ran out along the farmhouse, right across the road, right through their ranks, taking them by surprise. This enabled us to get 50yd away in the dark before they started shooting at us as we ran along the ditch to battalion HQ.

We found our outfit heading back toward Bastogne and were happy to be with them.

At that time, I learned that we four had achieved a real accomplishment. That our battalion was able to withdraw when the tanks had moved back.

Captain Towns, our company commander (who was killed on 26 December), came over and congratulated me on knocking out the tank, then reminded me that he had promised a pass to Paris to any soldier in his outfit if they knocked out a tank.

On 26 December, my best buddy Jack Gresh was killed. On the 28th, Sergeant Bowen was put out of commission with a loss of hearing and later captured. On the same day, Horkay lost a thumb, and that evening I was shot in the face, which ended my part in the Battle of the Bulge.

A check of decorations in the back of the 101st's official history indicates that despite his heroic actions, Lott received only the "citation" mentioned in his narrative. No medal for valor was awarded, yet most readers will probably agree that his action deserved at least the Silver Star.

Christmas Morning on the West Perimeter

Elements of the 15th Panzer-Grenadiers had massed for an all-out attempt to break into Bastogne from the west on Christmas Eve—actually 0300hr on Christmas morning. A concerted infantry attack actually broke into the A/502 lines at Champs and fighting from house to house went on through most of the night.

Sergeant Willis Fowler of that company had for some unknown reason, completely stripped and cleaned his LMG the day before. On the night of the attack he found himself on the flank of the German infantry thrust, firing belt after belt from a position near a potato house. The Germans were not aware of his location, and he took a heavy toll of them. Some actual hand-to-hand fighting was reported in the houses in Champs, and other 1/502 companies were shifted to meet the threat.

During that bleak night before Christmas, a German officer of the attack element found himself in

Mexican Pete
A Hispanic member of the 502, noted on the back of the photo only as "Mexican Pete," mans an LMG on the northwest section of the perimeter. *Krochka*

the Champs schoolhouse. While there, he quickly scribbled a poignant message on the chalkboard, which was discovered when the schoolmaster returned later. The message was as follows:

Let the world never see such a Christmas night again. To die far from one's children, one's wife and mother, under fire of guns, there is no greater cruelty.

To take away from his mother a son, a husband from his wife, a father from his children, is it worthy of a human being? Life can only be for love and respect.

At the sight of ruins, of blood and death, universal fraternity will rise.

A German Officer

By 0600, the 502 had launched a counterattack to drive the Germans from the houses they held for only 3hr. By 0800, the town was cleared and the lo-cals counted some 99 German bodies and many more wounded in the area. Whether the author of the above sentiment survived is unknown.

Sergeant Fowler had fired 6–10 belts (250 rounds per belt) of ammo through his machine gun. Because of his crucial role in decimating the enemy attackers, Fowler was awarded the Silver Star. When a request was made for an infantryman to represent the 101st Airborne on a Paris radio program called Combat Diary, Fowler's name was submitted by his first sergeant, and he departed on 26 December for Paris. Also going to record the show for broadcast to the states were General McAuliffe, a medic, and an artilleryman.

To the south of Champs, a large German task force spearheaded by 17 tanks (mostly Mark IV's with at least one Panther in the group), broke through the lines of the 401 and A/327. Some of the tanks were hit by 75mm howitzers, bazooka fire, and small arms fire. They menaced the CP of Lt. Col. Ray Allen, CO of the 401, and he fled on foot, making his escape and nearly being gunned down by men of the 502 as he approached their line on foot.

Tank destroyers contributed to the whittling down of the German tank force as did Colonel Cooper's 75mms of the 463rd PFAB. The German in-

This crossroads near Champs, Belgium, was photographed by Lt. David White of regimental S-2 of the 502.

A KO'd Panther tank knocked out in the northwest sector. *Krochka*

Lead Scout
Corporal Newman Tuttle (left, S-2 patrol lead scout) with Sgt. Gordon Little and Sgt. Graham Armstrong on the road to Bastogne on 30 December 1944. *White*

fantry, in at least battalion strength, had fallen behind the rampaging tanks and were mowed down in a terrific crossfire from machine guns of the 401. A number of .50cal guns had been retrieved by the glidermen, still in cosmoline, near Crossroad X a few days earlier. These were cross-fired in such a devastating manner that the Germans fell atop each other in heaps. After breaking through, the surviving German armor spread out, one tank driving up into Champs and others menacing the 502 CP at Rolle. Cooks, clerks, and radiomen of the 377 and other units fell out in the snow with rifles to stop the holiday breakthrough.

At the Rolle chateau, 502nd demolitions sergeant Schuyler Jackson armed himself with a bazooka and crept forward to KO the leading enemy tank. Twenty-five years later, Schuyler returned to the spot and told a reporter from the *Army Digest*:

> This is really a strange feeling to be standing here now. Five tanks had broken through. Four had already been hit when the fifth was coming by me. I was behind this tree. Right after it passed, I stepped out and let him have it with my bazooka. It went a few more yards, then went off the road up there where you see that bale of hay. The Germans came tearing out of that tank; let me tell you, they were ready to fight. We shot them down.

Sky Jackson won the Silver Star for this action, and Sgt. Gordon Little was down the road where another tank had gone off the road into a ditch. It too was hit by a bazooka rocket, which "buzzed around inside." The German commander was killed when he climbed out of the turret.

None of the 17 German tanks that broke through that day made it back to the enemy lines. The tank that broke into Champs was destroyed by

Hitching a Ride
Members of the 502 catch a jeep ride in the snow, near
Rolle, Belgium. *via Swartz*

Aerial Lifeline
Another perspective on the glorious day of aerial resupply on 23 December. This photo was made near Savy, Belgium, where guns of the 377 were emplaced. *Benecke*

bazooka fire from John Ballard of A/502. Ballard shot the rocket into the tank's engine compartment after it passed about 15yd from his position. (Ballard was KIA on 4 January, 1945.) Sergeant Charles Asay and S/Sgt. Willis Zweibel captured 25 Germans in Champs; the Germans had been hiding behind a woodpile.

Later in the afternoon of Christmas Day a lone tank that had hidden somewhere inside the American perimeter made a mad dash to get back to German lines. It too was knocked out and became known as the "Maverick Tank." The west perimeter by Christmas afternoon was decorated with numerous knocked-out tanks and some halftracks, plus numerous German corpses. Some of the German dead had fallen beside their tanks, and Len Swartz of the 502 said, "I'll never forget the sight of the red blood on that white snow."

Another detail remembered by Swartz was that one of the knocked-out German tanks was staffed by two female Panzer women, who were crying as they climbed out into captivity. Swartz saw them taken away for interrogation.

After Patton's Third Army had broken the circle around Bastogne, Patton himself came to visit the west perimeter and reportedly derived great enjoyment from viewing the numerous tanks and infantry stopped in the 502 sector. He arrived personally at the Rolle CP to decorate Lt. Col. Steve Chappuis who had just gone to sleep after being awake for several days and nights. The sleepy Chappuis stood to attention as his DSC was pinned on, and after some words of congratulations, Patton left. Although the 502 had played a key role on

Bringing in German prisoners on the west perimeter.

Christmas Day, the majority of tanks were knocked out by other outfits. It is ironic that they were not able to share in much of the credit.

More Christmas Action

One of the engagements fought by the 502 on the west perimeter was described in the official *Combat Lessons No. 6*. The company described is C/502:

Leadership Is Aggressive

The value of aggressive action even against superior enemy forces is again illustrated by this story of a small group of men from the 502nd Parachute Infantry Regiment, as recounted by Private First Class William Reubendael: "At daylight, Christmas morning, one group of 20 men encountered a German company of about 150 men supported by 4

Battalion COs Pow-Wow
Conference of battalion COs of the 502 at Bastogne, circa January 1945: Lt. Col. Thomas Sutliffe (2/502), Lt. Col. John Stopka (3/502), and Lt. Col. "Long John Hanlon (1/502). Stopka was killed by mistake in an attack by P-47 fighters on 14 January 1945. *Musura*

Mark IV tanks. The Americans had 4 light machine guns, 2 bazookas, and their rifles and carbines.

The Germans were already digging-in when discovered. Their tanks soon opened fire on the farmhouse around which the Americans had taken positions and forced our men back about 200yd to the edge of a patch of woods. At that point the hard-pressed platoon leader decided that his best defense was bold attack. He borrowed several riflemen from a nearby company and then had his MGs keep the enemy infantry down and their tanks buttoned up while the two bazooka teams and the riflemen moved around to the German company's flank. This small but aggressive maneuvering force inflicted heavy casualties upon the enemy infantry, knocked out three tanks, and forced the other tank to withdraw, to a point where it was totally destroyed by another American unit. Not content with this accomplishment, the paratroopers moved on to attack a nearby enemy-held farmhouse. The German occupants surrendered, turning over their weapons to some American prisoners they had been holding in the same building."

A Tragic Accident

Members of the 502's regimental demolitions platoon had devised and rigged up a fiendish booby trap in the woods near a stream, some distance from their CP This consisted of a clump of C-2 plastic explosive, embedded with horseshoes, nails, and assorted scrap metal—all planted against the base of a tree with a tripwire ignition system.

Although the location was known, it was not precisely marked, which would lead to a tragedy.

On 28 December, a recon patrol was sent in the vicinity of the boobytrap. Because HQ was aware of the booby trap's presence in the vicinity, a guide was sent along with the S-2 men to make sure they avoided it. This guide was a new replacement, who had only recently joined the 502.

When the patrol reached the vicinity of the trap, the guide appeared uncertain of precisely where it was located. Then, seeing the stream, he remarked, "Now I know, it's over there."

"Let's move out," said Bob Paczulla, who was leading the patrol.

Just then, a member of the patrol must have kicked the tripwire. There was a horrible blast, and Pvt. Louis P. Migliarese, a close friend of Paczulla's

Digging their Own Graves?
Len Swartz recorded this photo of POWs digging a straddle trench. He said, "The Italian guards told the Krauts that they were Jewish. The Germans probably thought they were digging their own graves." *Swartz*

dropped with a mortal wound. Another trooper received multiple fragments in his legs, but survived. Paczulla was also hit.

Devastated by the death of his friend in this tragic accident, Paczulla carried Mig's personal effects back to the Rolle castle, found his way into the chapel, and prayed for his dead friend.

A demotions lieutenant apologized to Bob for the mistake, "But it didn't bring Migliarese back," said Paczulla.

Teamwork

In many ETO battles, the TD had proven less successful than anticipated in its role of knocking out enemy armor. The vulnerability of these vehicles to counterfire was demonstrated again and again during the battles at Bastogne. The M-10 TD was most numerous.

Among the TDs caught in the Bastogne encirclement were M7B1 Priest mounting a 105 howitzer

Christmas Morning Hero
Sergeant Willis Fowler of A/502 (center) was the Christmas morning hero at Champs, Belgium. He won the Silver Star and went to Paris for a *Combat Diary* interview. *Glenn Johnson*

and the new M18 Hellcat mounting a 76mm gun. Some of these vehicles belonged to the 705th TD Bn.

The original concept of deploying TDs was to send them out in search of enemy armor. But experience had proven they did better lying in wait in a defensive role.

The TDs fared somewhat better in this role but despite success in taking out enemy tanks as at Marvie or on the west perimeter, they always seemed to lose some of their own vehicles to retaliatory enemy fire. Teamwork and improvisation was called for in each situation.

Combat Lessons No. 6 contained the following example of such improvised use of teamwork, although the specific units and locations are not given:

Locating Enemy Tanks at Night

Suggested by the Assistant G-2, 101st Airborne Division: "At night, we placed a machine gun on both sides of a TD. When hostile tanks were heard approaching, the machine guns fired tracers until ricochets indicated that a tank was being hit. Both guns would then fire at the tank and the TD would fire at the "V" formed by the converging machine gun tracers."

B/502 had repulsed one major German attack and shifted to a ridge overlooking open ground on the right of A/502. Some distance behind them was Champs, and Longchamps was situated to their right rear.

Sergeant Forest Jay Nichols had established his squad on this crest and had a .50cal machine gun on the left of his squad. The weapon had been salvaged from another unit and had a bent top plate. The troopers had repaired it and used it in their defensive position. More unusual was the British Bren gun they had set up on the right edge of their squad. Jay Nichols had found the gun at Elst, Holland, on the Island, had brought it back to Mourmelon with a good supply of ammo. These weapons proved to be a superb supplement to their rifles and Tommy-guns.

On New Years Eve, after dark, Jay went back to Champs to get some K-rations for his men. He went from foxhole to foxhole, handing the food down to the men. As he was kneeling above one hole, a terrific German artillery barrage began. A shell exploded near Nichols, and he fell with multiple wounds atop the man in the hole. Doc Archie treated Nichols and found wounds on his face, left arm, left hand, and left side. The war was over for Nichols, but he

A German corpse is searched for valuables by members of an artillery unit west of Bastogne. *Krochka*

would survive. Corporal Milton S. Lowry, his assistant squad leader, was killed by the same barrage.

Later in January, as troops of the 17th Airborne and 35th and 87th Inf. moved up. The 101st troops on the west perimeter would move north and east, toward Bourcy and Houffalize.

Chapter Seventeen

Longchamps and Monaville

The word Longchamps means "Long Fields" in French, and members of 2/502 will never forget the area north of the town where they formed their defensive perimeter. The town itself lies near the northwest corner of the circular Bastogne defense line, and the area north of the town is characterized by a huge valley. A single road runs from the town northbound, into the valley and continues northward up the far side and beyond. The 2/502 dug in on the higher ground on the south edge of the valley, facing north. F/502 was on the left (west side of the road, with the remaining companies strung out to the east toward the next village (Monaville). From Monaville east, was the 3/502, whose line extended as far as Recogne, where it tied-in with G/506.

"I Don't Need Any Company. I'm From Chicago!"

Germans trying to find a way into Bastogne didn't get around to trying the Longchamps area until late December. The first sizable contact may have been with a two-man F/502 LP late one night near Christmas.

Frank Tiedeman and Howard Matthews took an LMG across the big valley and set up a LP in the woods near the road. In the darkness, they became aware that a lone trooper from another company was dug-in on the other side of the road.

"Hey, why don't you come over here and join us?," Frank called to him.

"I don't need any company. I'm from Chicago!" the lone trooper replied, staying put in his position.

Around 0400hr, the Americans heard the sound of hobnailed boots marching toward them. An entire company of Germans was marching toward them in neat columns, unaware of their presence. Holding fire until the head of the column was abreast of their position, Tiedeman and Matthews opened-up with the LMG, taking the large enemy force totally by surprise. The lone trooper across the road also fired his rifle as fast as possible. The stunned German survivors retreated, seeking a different approach to Longchamps.

In the light of dawn, the Americans found several dozen German bodies lying on the road. They withdrew to the front-line.

The Attack of 3 January

A number of patrols and skirmishes took place in this area before the main German effort hit on 3 January when a coordinated and concerted drive to break into Bastogne from the northeast and northwest simultaneously was planned by the Germans. The attack on Longchamps would be launched by the 19th SS Panzer-Grenadier Reg. of the 9th SS Panzer Div. This unit had opposed the 101st at the dike positions across from Renkum in Holland.

On the night of 2 January, a German runner mistakenly walked up to a foxhole of 2/502 in the darkness and asked a question in German. He was punched in the face by Lincoln Bethel of the 502 and was captured by Bethel and Reg Davies. They took the prisoner back to HQ/502 for questioning and Rene Schmidt, the interpreter, informed them that this was perhaps the most valuable prisoner taken

Silver Star
Franklin "Ray" Blasingame (left) won a Silver Star on 3 January 1945 at Longchamps for knocking out two tanks with his bazooka. At right is his pal Willard Davis. *Sapinski*

Monaville
German prisoners being brought into town east of Longchamps on 17 January 1945. *White*

by the 101st in WWII. For this runner had maps and details of the attack plan of his regiment, scheduled for the following day. Armed with this information, the Americans called artillery concentrations into the staging areas of the 9th SS and were able to disrupt and weaken the coming attack.

This was most fortunate because, even in a diminished state, the 19th SS made a devastating attack against 2/502 on 3 January.

Lawrence Silva, manning a radio, first reported German tanks moving up. During his last transmission, a German tank was parked directly over his hole. His body was found later. He had no marks on him and had presumably died as a result of carbon monoxide poisoning from the exhaust of the tank.

When the tanks and panzer-grenadiers did come in, they hit D/502 on the right side of the highway first, threatening to break the line near Monaville. German tanks stopped and pivoted over individual foxholes, crushing the paratroopers inside with their tracks. Part of F/502 was sent across the road to help D.

Here, Calfboy Blasingame of F/502 was able to hit a half dozen German tanks at point-blank range with his bazooka, although most of the rockets deflected or failed to explode.

Bert Ellard served as loader for Calfboy, and the pair did succeed in knocking out two of the tanks. For this, Blasingame was awarded the Silver Star. Ellard also lived to tell about it. He recalled that some of these "tanks" were actually self-propelled guns, thus they couldn't aim their main batteries without turning the entire chassis of the vehicle. This may have helped Ellard and Blasingame to avoid large-caliber counterfire.

Over on the west side of the highway, crack shots were decimating the Germans as they came in masses on foot. The panzer troops had more men than tanks, so they used some of their panzer crewmen as infantry, advancing across the snowy white valley in their stark black tunics.

They ran forward with zeal in the belief that they were coming through, but the Americans mowed them down. Numerous analogies have been drawn between the defense of the Alamo and the siege of Bastogne. Here on this ground above Longchamps, the comparison was perhaps a good one. When the shooting stopped, the valley floor was dotted with black uniformed panzer troops and the nearest one to Joe Pistone's hole lay only 3ft away!

East of the road, it was chaos. The battle was not going well for the 502, and Hans Sannes of D/502 was among those who lay wounded, with German tanks passing close to his position. He lay expecting to die, but like many others found himself still among the living when the German troops withdrew. Guns of the 321 helped stop the 19th SS.

Over 40 members of F/502 were wounded and captured by the SS troopers, no doubt the largest number of 101st men ever captured right off a front-line in any battle of WWII. Frank Tiedeman and Howie Matthews had left to get ammo in a jeep. They drove back into the line just in time to be captured. As the Germans lined them up, American artillery fire came in, wounding a number of friendly troops, including Tiedeman, who was sprayed in the face, arms, and body with shrapnel. Earl Hendricks, the company commander was shot in the arm and also captured. Blasingame, Ellard, and 1st Sgt. Les Harder, managed to escape along with a third of the company.

Chapter Eighteen

Recogne and Bourcy

The hamlet of Recogne, Belgium, lies several miles north of Bastogne. Company G/506 dug in in the woods facing Recogne from the south. There, in snowy foxholes, they would suffer the effects of the weather, perhaps more so than the other units, as there were no farmhouses in or behind their line to rotate into for warmth. The men did build a huge bonfire on Christmas Eve and miraculously received no German fire despite the glow, which was no doubt visible for hundreds of yards.

The Overcoat with 22 Bullet Holes

In the area west of Recogne, H/502 had put a forward LP in an isolated clump of pine trees in front of their front line. In this post were three troopers manning an LMG. One night, German tanks were heard in the area, so at dawn 1st Sgt. Harry Bush walked to the forward post with a bazooka and two rookie replacements to provide more firepower to the LP.

Unknown to the three Americans as they walked forward, the men in the LP had fallen asleep and had just been captured by a German patrol. The three German intruders had them face down on the ground when Bush's group approached.

Bush gave a low whistle at the clump of pines and said "Sgt. Bush coming in"

He was greeted by a fusillade of 9mm bullets, coming from the trees. Bush unslung his Tommy-gun and returned fire. Machine-pistol slugs nipped his overcoat and dropped the two men beside him. Bush sprayed the trees with one clip, loaded anoth-

er, and continued spraying. Return fire had diminished by the time he was firing the third magazine. Bush noticed that the hot bore of his Thompson barrel had expanded and the slugs had no velocity in coming out the muzzle. He could see them dropping before they even reached the trees. Slinging the submachine gun on his shoulder, he produced his .45 pistol and emptied that into the trees also. Finally, 1st Sgt. Bush walked forward, aware that his right arm was bleeding. One slug had hit him between the elbow and shoulder.

It was quiet as he parted the branches and saw three Germans down. Two were dead, the third was badly wounded and on his knees. Bush grabbed the Thompson with both hands behind the front sight and swung it downward like a club, smashing the wooden stock over the helmet of the wounded German.

The captured outpost men were still alive. They took Bush to a field hospital where his overcoat was removed. In the skirt and arms of the coat, the medics counted 22 9mm bullet holes; eleven slugs had passed through making two holes each. Only one slug had hit Bush.

"Mein Kopf!"

After one of the evening attacks against G/506, German bodies were strewn across the open ground in front of Recogne. One of the Germans kept screaming "Mein Kopf! Mein Kopf!" ("My head," in German)

Ed Slizewski heard one of his buddies comment "That fanatical Kraut bastard—he's dying and he's

Killed at Recogne
Pfc. Charles Merritts of F/501 was the best friend of Leo Gillis. Merritts was killed in F Company's tragic attack on Recogne. *Gillis*

Heroic Medic
Combat Medic Irving "Blackie" Baldinger of H/506. Admired by all in his company, Blackie showed great courage in carrying wounded buddies from bullet-swept open fields near Recogne. *Andros*

yelling 'Mein Kampf.'" Finally, Pee Wee Martin saw one of the men walk out with a .45, saying "I'm tired of listening to him; he's not going to make it anyways."

A pistol shot ended the yelling.

Other Attacks

One of the worst barrages came in when a few TDs pulled in behind the company front-line.

"We hated to see them because they always attracted the German artillery," said Pee Wee Martin.

As shells came flying in, the men got low in their holes, and one of Pee Wee's friends, Sgt. Dean Christensen, got behind and under a TD, thinking it was the safest place to be. But a mortar shell landed right behind the TD and shrapnel killed Christensen.

The heaviest German attack saw a battalion-size infantry unit with tank support drive against the G/506 line. In the face of this, most of the men left their positions and fell back, to be stopped by an officer 200yd to the rear. One machine-gunner, Stan

Clever, who had been captured in Normandy but escaped, never received the word to withdraw. He wasn't aware of being alone, but he also didn't consider being captured again an option. Clever singlehandedly mowed down many Germans and held the line until his buddies returned to their positions. He was reportedly a bit angry that he had been left alone on the firing line. This intrepid act was recognized only with a Bronze Star.

Sometime in January, Pee Wee Martin observed a patrol from H/506 make an assault across a snowy field near Recogne. The snow was knee deep but an icy crust had formed on the surface. It was possible to walk some distance, breaking through the surface only occasionally.

The lead scouts of the group were cut down by machine-gun fire, and a dark-haired medic nearby began stripping off his musette bag and webbing.

"What are you doing?," Pee Wee asked him.

"I'm the medic; it's my job to go out and get them."

"Well hell, you'll be killed . . . you're not going to help anyone that way."

The medic took off running across the open area and dragged and carried two wounded men back, one at a time, across the cruel, icy, exposed field.

The medic, "Blackie" Baldinger, survived. Blackie was another unsung hero who was not rec-

Smiling Mortarman
An 81mm mortarman of the 501 at Foy, Belgium, 1945.
Signal Corps

Peaceful Pines
A classic view of snow-laden pines near Bastogne.
Krochka

ognized with a medal for his heroic acts. He passed away in the early 1990s. His son served in combat with the 101st Airborne in the Vietnam War.

The hamlet of Recogne had changed hands several times by 9 January, but on that day, it was being held by the Germans. A plan was laid to bring F/501 around to assault and re-take the town from the south entrance.

The night before F/501's attack, a wire-laying team had walked right into the town in the dark, then realized their predicament and dropped the wire spool on the road and ran back. Thus, during the following day's attack, the German commander could have hooked onto the wire and conferred with the American commander had he been so inclined.

During daylight, F/501 left the treeline that had been home so long for G/506, came down the hill, and approached Recogne. Third Platoon came right up along the road from the south. First Platoon had almost reached the first buildings when the Germans opened up and pinned them down.

Sergeant Bass, caught in the open, was screaming "Get 'em offa my back!" He ran to the shelter of a chicken coop. But Art Lufkin was caught on the open ground, wounded. Nine slugs eventually tore into his jaw, neck, back, and legs, but he survived. While he lay wounded, a hog trotted over and began to nibble at his wounds. Art's buddies shot the pig, which fell between him and the Germans, offering some concealment at last.

During the attack, Gillis' best friend, Charles Merritts, was fatally wounded.

Under command of acting CO Clair Hess, F/501 rampaged into the town. A single sniper on the approach had killed a number of men and O'Neill thinks the sniper was among those killed in the first house, but this will never be known for certain. Company E came up to assist F/501 in clearing the houses, but Lt. Joe McGregor was shot in the head a second time while crossing the road. This time, the wound was fatal.

In all, 25 men and three officers were lost by E and F Companies in the taking of Recogne. Col. Julian Ewell, commander of the 501 PIR, was seriously wounded on 10 January and had to be replaced by Robert A. Ballard. Ballard commanded the 501st until its deactivation after V-E Day.

Around 10 January, the entire 501 had been moved to the area north of Bastogne. The woods in the Foy-Bizory-Fazone areas were still being cleared of German troops. Bill Russo of C/501 recalled an episode from that period:

We had a lieutenant in C/501 named Grimaldi—Alfonso Grimaldi. He was with the coast artillery in New York City, then he joined the parachute troops. He joined us as a first lieutenant replacement.

Attack on Bourcy, 16 December
Lieutenant David White of the HQ/502 S-2 section recorded this scene of the attack. Germans vacated the town just before American troops entered. *White*

You Found a Home in the Army, Chum!
Looking like a scene from the movie *Battleground*, this is an actual view of troopers sheltering during an artillery barrage. *Krochka*

Over to the left of us was a very thin woods, sticking out like a peninsula. Three sides were exposed to German fire . . . and they told Grimaldi to go clear that woods. That was *murder*, what happened to him. He led a patrol in there, and not one of them got out. Not a man . . . not one.

Later in January, the 502 pushed northeast along the railroad line through Jack's Woods, toward the town of Bourcy. The 327 was nearby, and 3/501 was still in position south of the railroad line. P-47 fighter-bombers gave close-in support, but with the confusion caused by the heavy forest close to both sides of the track, the inevitable happened. The 3/502 was crossing a small snowy clearing when some P-47's swooped down and dropped bombs on a group. Major John P. Stopka, who had won the DSC in Colonel Cole's bayonet charge at Carentan, was among the men killed.

Lieutenant Felix Stanley looked into the field from G/501 positions and saw a number of badly wounded troopers bouncing on the field in their death throes. A brief truce was called, and medics of both sides appeared to collect the wounded and dead. Also in that area, Leo Pichler, an original member of the 502 and a member of the boxing team, was killed right on the railroad line while putting out aerial recognition panels. Total losses that day numbered 12 dead and 25 wounded.

When the town of Bourcy was finally assaulted, the Germans pulled out, leaving the town to the US Army.

Chapter Nineteen

The Bitch Bulge—Alsace-Lorraine

Since early January, a smaller version of the German Bulge had been pushed against Gen. Jacob Devers' Seventh Army in the south sector of the western front. The Alsace-Lorraine area that lies north of the Vosges Mountains and south of the Black Forest, had changed hands numerous times in wars between Germany and France. Half the populace spoke French, and the rest spoke German. The loyalties of the civilian population were questionable.

The sector facing the Moder River near Hagenau had been held by the 42nd Inf. Div. The 101st was trucked directly from Bastogne to this Moder River front to bolster the line where the Germans had pushed through. Because of the proximity of the area to the German town of Bitschhoffen, the 501 began to refer to this campaign as "The Bitch Bulge." This also reflected their attitude at being sent there from Bastogne, instead of to a rest area.

Lieutenant Sefton of 2/501 described the trip:

> We boarded the Air Corps vans with no roofs on them, and that ride of some 200 miles was probably the most miserable experience of the entire Battle of the Bulge for us. We were in those things, stamping our feet on the steel beds, trying to keep from freezing. The trucks were so thoroughly uncomfortable, and the pace was so great, that everybody on that trip suffered terribly. Our morale was already pretty low. I had gone into Bastogne with 40 men in the platoon, and there were only 14 of us left, counting the mortar squad—and that was not an abnormally shrunken unit.

> We had lost a lot of people, and those who were left were feeling pretty much that the war was a lousy business and that we had been ill-used, and we were hardly cheering about the fact of going down and trying to pull chestnuts out of the fire in another area.

Upon arrival in the sector on 26 January 1945, the 327 and 501 relieved the 222nd Inf. Reg., which had taken heavy casualties when German troops attacked across the river. They left many of their dead lying in the snow, until a plea was made to their commander to come and remove them. The 42nd Inf. Div. men used to paint little signs with a facsimile of their rainbow patch and the words "The Rainbow Division was here." Members of the 501 obtained some paint and wrote next to their graffiti: "Where the hell are you now?"

The initial 101st line faced north across the Moder River from Hagenau to Neuborg, a front of about 4 miles. On one flank was the 79th Div. and on the other the 103rd Cactus Div., recently taken over by General McAuliffe of "Nuts" fame.

Operation Oscar

Company A/501 had lost two commanders recently. Captain Stach had been sent back to the states as last surviving male in his family. Lieutenant Charlie Seale had been accidentally shot to death in the woods north of Bastogne. Lieutenant Hugo Sims, of Incredible Patrol fame was sent to A/501 as its new commander. The company was given the honor of leading the only significant incur-

Divarty to Alsace
This truck, bearing markings of the 377th PFAB, actually contains members of the 101st's Division Artillery unit as they headed to Alsace-Lorraine from the Bulge. Left to right: Landrum, J. Miller, Necikowski, Powell, Cahill, O'Shaughnessy, Dilloway, Town, R. Miller, Clarence Theaker. *Theaker*

sion across the Moder River in Operation Oscar, a raid conducted the night of 31 January to 1 February. Also participating was B/501 and E/327. Engineers of B/326 installed two footbridges cross the Moder near Neuborg.

Ed Hallo, operations sergeant for A/501 gives a brief account of his company's role in the raid:

We walked right across this frozen river—it was wintertime. Company B crossed in another area. We went over about 1,000–1,500yd behind the lines. I had to run up to Sims. I said, "Captain, slow down! You're losing your men back here!"

He didn't know the men in the company, and he had given orders that if anybody got wounded, they're to make it back on their own—don't stop to help anybody out. So we went up there, we got along a road, and these Germans came up in platoon formation, "links-links-links . . ." When they got in the middle of us, we let loose and we slaughtered them.

In the meantime, Ed Gulick of the third platoon got shot. "We'll pick him up on the way back," Sims said. "Let's go." And he took off. When we all went back, I told the guys to pick up Gulick. We picked him up, put his body in a raincoat, and carried him back . . . didn't find out until after we got him back that he was dead.

I walked right into battalion HQ with Lieutenant Sims and they pinned the Silver Star on him.

He turned to me and said "Hallo, this won't get you the Silver Star, but I don't know what I would've done without you."

I didn't say anything, and you could've heard a pin drop. This guy, every time you turned around, he got a medal.

Later, when we got to tent city at Mourmelon le Petit, some of the replacements got a furlough and went to Paris. I was an original member of the company and hadn't had a furlough yet. Sims took off for Paris and left word with the executive officer: "Don't let Hallo go on furlough."

Chow Cart
Using a farm cart as dining room table, members of A/377 dine in Alsace. *Benecke*

Seasoned Warrior
Ken Casler, who had fought in assorted 1/501 companies from Hell's Corners to Bastogne, sits in his hole in Alsace. *Sloan*

Happy Warrior
Waldo Brown, a member of HQ/501's S-2 section. His portrait was made in Alsace by Gopher Sloan. *via Wilbur*

I complained to the EXO that some of the men were going on their second round of furloughs. He said, "I can't help it, Hallo. Sims says not to let you go, and I've got to follow orders."

The net results of Operation Oscar for the 501 were five killed, eight wounded, and three missing. Company B's 1st Sgt. Joe Henderson was among those killed. One German officer and 20 enlisted prisoners were brought back.

The 327 lost one man killed, 13 wounded, and one missing. They captured one German officer and 15 enlisted men.

Numerous lesser-known patrols went across the Moder River during this period, the patrols always careful not to cross twice at the same spot. Troopers like Tex McMorries of G/501 prowled the German rear and became like hunters. Don Burgett returned from one patrol by wading across the Moder River. He found it was only waist deep in that spot.

New replacement Ken Parker of C/506 observed the survivors of the Bastogne fighting. He recalled, "None of them talked much; they all looked extremely exhausted, and they were all absolutely

Mess Line
Mess line in Hagenau or Neuborg area was recorded by Jim Duggins of HQ/501. *Duggins*

The Club Mobile
A Red Cross wagon dispenses coffee and donuts in Alsace, February, 1945. *Duggins*

filthy dirty—every inch of their uniforms. Apparently, in Bastogne, they'd never had a chance to change or wash or do much of anything except eat and survive."

Fearless or Crazy? A Dinner At Neubourg

Some of the troopers in rifle companies were fortunate to have the shelter of homes in the Moder River area. By scrounging and using 10-in-1 rations, the combat troops could sometimes concoct a sizable meal.

The following incident as related by Tex McMorries of G/501 gives an insight into the death-defying humor which was characteristic of some of the more-fearless troopers:

A bunch of guys prepared a feast. We had the food on a table in Neubourg [Alsace], when suddenly German artillery started coming in. One round tore a corner out of the house. All the level-headed guys went to the cellar—also two or three officers with them . . .

I don't know whose idea it was, but Frank Serawatka and I decided what a joke it would be to go ahead and eat. So with everyone else deep in the cellar (where we should have been), Serawatka and myself sat down at the table. With artillery raking the town and a couple more rounds tearing into the house, plaster falling in our food, dust filling the room, we sat at the table, enjoying the food, the joke, and watching the bricks jump and dust fly as the rounds pounded Neuborg—just like a ringside seat.

Also, we enjoyed kidding about the German gunners: Should we go make a deal for them to fire every day at mealtime? Or should there be blood on the moon tonight (a common expression we used), and should we revoke their licenses to fire those big

133

Tough Hombre
"Ridgerunner" Jimmy Edgar of I/501, inflicts pain on a comrade at Camp Toccoa. After being wounded in battle and then told to go home after recovery by his CO, Bill Morgan, he replied, "Lieutenant, I've kicked sand in three dyin' company commanders' ass. I'll be back to kick sand in yours." And he did return. *Edgar*

Letter of Death
Oscar T. Sanders of HQ/2 501's 81mm mortar platoon sends another letter of death to Herman the German from a sandbagged dugout in Alsace. *via Tuel*

Strolling Through the Alsace
This photo of a typical scene in an Alsatian town was made by Al Krochka. *Krochka*

guns because of their bad manners firing at mealtime? Of course, you know what the permit revoking means.

Mean as a Rattlesnake

Sergeant Jimmy Edgar, an original member of I/501, who was mean as a rattlesnake, got wounded while in Alsace. His company commander, Lt. Bill Morgan came to say goodbye as Edgar was being loaded onto a stretcher.

"Sergeant Edgar," Morgan said, "why don't you take advantage of this wound and go back to the States. You've done more than your share."

Edgar's eyes narrowed and he replied, "Lieutenant, I've kicked sand in three dying company commanders' asses, and I'll be back to kick sand in yours!"

"Want a Light?"

A team of 101 pathfinders jumped at Prun, Germany, to signal a resupply drop of gasoline for the 4th Armored Div. For a few of them, like Lt. Schrable Williams, it was their fourth combat jump in WWII.

George "Frenchy" Blain had helped mark the DZ, then moved to the edge of the field designated as the DZ for the resupply. Near the edge of the field, he saw a jeep parked with two field-grade armored officers standing up in it, watching the approach of the C-47 resupply planes.

Blain approached and saluted them.

"Major, it might be a good idea for you to back that jeep away from the DZ. Some of the loads have been known to break loose and come down like a bomb."

The armored major removed the field glasses from his eyes and "looked at me like I was dog shit," said Blain.

"OK," said Blain. "Suit yourselves." The arrogant officers never said a word but continued to observe the resupply mission.

Ungrateful Dead
"The dead always looked so damned uncomfortable, you wanted to readjust their bodies," said Don Burgett. He was speaking of men like this Luftwaffe ground division soldier killed in Alsace, who lies twisted in death. *Benecke*

Hagenau, 31 January 1945
Privates Arno Whitbread and Martin Chisholm (behind gun) of 1/327 with a scrounged .50cal MG, commanding an approach to Hagenau. The MG's muzzle is covered until ready to fire to keep snow out of the barrel. *Signal Corps*

Off to the Front
A member of 1st Platoon, F/501, going to the front line in
Alsace. *Korvas*

As the parachuted bundles of jerry cans were
kicked out of the planes, one can broke loose, came
down at full speed and hit the front end of the jeep.
The can burst open, splashing gasoline all over the
occupants and the vehicle.

Frenchy walked over to them, produced his
Zippo lighter, and asked, "Want a light?"

Survivors
Survivors of Wardin from I/501 were captured on film in Al-
sace by the camera of Billy Ogle. Left to right: Johnson,
Ogle, Welch, Turner, and Higgins. *Ogle*

Chapter Twenty

"40 & 8s" to Mourmelon le Petit

In late February, the 101st Airborne Div. was pulled out of Alsace and loaded onto WWI-vintage French railroad boxcars known as "40 & 8s" because they were the right size to hold 40 men or eight horses. A lengthy train ride carried them south to the Reims area once again, to the smaller of the two Mourmelon towns. An advance guard had departed ahead of the rest of the division to set up a huge tent city using German POWs for labor. The

Airborne Railroad
Boxcars like this transported the 101st Airborne from Alsace to Mourmelon le Petit. From top down: Ken Collier, Bill Canfield, Smoky Ladman, Frank Sayers, Frank Castiglione, Roland J. Wilbur, Joe Sloan, and an unknown trooper. *Sloan*

"40 & 8" Boxcars
Sergeant Ted Vetland and Luke Easley of A/506 haul hay to line the floor of the railroad car that will carry them from Alsace to Mourmelon le Petit. Note the bandages on their right shoulders, which conceal the eagle patches for security reasons. *Kennedy*

Cannon Cockers
Artillerymen of A/377 rode the same way. This group was captured on film by Ed Benecke. *Benecke*

Mourmelon le Petit, Spring 1945
Left to right: Maj. R. J. Allen, Col. Robert Ballard (CO of the 501), unknown, Lt. Col. Sammie Homan, Brereton, Maj. Ray Bottomly, and Maj. Doug Davidson. *Duggins*

troopers would once again reside in M34 pyramidal tents like those used in many parts of England before D-day.

Allen Hurd, a member of 2/501's S-2 section, described the train trip in a letter to his parents:

We came back to France to base camp on freight cars. We rode first class. First class in France means "40 & 8" boxcars with hay on the floors. Plenty of fresh air and good opportunity to give the countryside the once-over when you ride these broken-down relics. We passed bridge after bridge demolished by our air force. Railroad cars and tank cars litter the side of the track. I know now what it

means when they say, "Our air force bombed the Marshalling yards at such and such a place." Believe me, they do a devastating job of it. In the fields of France, you can read the history of the war. Foxholes, thousands of them, forests split and torn by artillery shells, burned-out vehicles of all descriptions, bomb craters, ration cans, ammunition boxes—all this and so much more shout their gruesome history at you as you pass by.

After arriving at Mourmelon, some men received furloughs and passes to Paris or other French tourist attractions, but the majority of men were sweating out the climactic final combat jump of the war, possibly into Berlin as part of the planned Operation Eclipse. For those who had been fighting since Bastogne without a break the delays in going to Paris were intolerable. Hurd also wrote of this situation:

Hurd, a lousy Pfc, protests to the world on the pass and furlough policy of the 101st Division. In

Line 'Em Up
Second Platoon of F/501 at tent city, Mourmelon le Petit.

Left to right: O'Neill, Bones Reed, Imhauser, Guthrie, Jumbo Moore, Toner, and others. *Hughes*

other words, why aren't I in Paris, instead of sitting in the woods of France. (The division was recently returned to same camp we were at when we were so rudely interrupted that fateful December morn.) Maxwell DAVENPORT Taylor, our commander, who at the time of the breakthrough was sojourning in Washington, said at the time, quote, "Well done!," as they placed the Christmas turkey before him. McAuliffe, our acting commander said at that time, while residing in the deepest cellar in Bastogne, said: "NUTS!" Now, while we watch C-47's practice their formation daily overhead, we "The Battered Bastards of Bastogne," without any furlough in sight want to say, "Nuts."

We are back off the stage, waiting and "sweating-out" our appearance in the climactic final act. If you don't hear from me for a long time, you'll know I'm in combat and a review of the papers will tell you where.

Presidential Citation

On a more optimistic note, on 15 March 1945 the entire 101st Div. was assembled on a field near Reims to receive a Presidential Citation for the de-

fense of Bastogne. It was the first time an entire division was so recognized. General Eisenhower made the speech and presentation, and it was a happy day for all.

Ike stated it was a "great personal honor" for him to present the award, which was the beginning of a new tradition in the US Army. Ike realized that some of the 101st soldiers who had fought in Normandy and Holland did not rate Bastogne as their toughest fight, but it was appropriate that the division should be cited for that battle. Being rushed in to hold that position was of utmost importance, and all the elements of battle drama were there. Ike attached the Presidential Distinguished Unit streamer to the division's flag, and the thousands of assembled troops marched past in review.

Training Continues

While at Mourmelon, a number of men from both A/501, E/501, and G/502, were killed in live-fire training. Johnny Altick, one of the youngest men in E/501—who had survived Normandy, Holland, and Bastogne—was hit by a burst of machine-gun fire at the end of a training problem and died. Lieutenant Jesus Cortez of G/502 was among those killed when some mortar rounds fell short on another training exercise.

"A Great Personal Honor"
Stating that it was a "great personal honor" for him, Gen.

Dwight Eisenhower presented the 101st Airborne with the Presidential Citation award on 15 March 1945. *Krochka*

To the Ruhr

On 24 March, the 101st watched C-47s take off carrying men of the 17th Airborne Div. toward Wesel, Germany, where they would make a combat jump across the Ruhr. This along with two other crossings of that German water barrier would set the stage for the commitment of the 101st to the Ruhr industrial area of Germany. In early April, the entire division, except for the 501, boarded trucks and headed north to hold the west edge of the so-called Ruhr Pocket near Dusseldorf, Germany.

The 501 would remain behind at Mourmelon where it was divided into teams to drop onto a number of German Stalags and Oflags to rescue Allied POW's from possible massacre by the dying Nazi regime. This mission, code-named Operation Jubliant, was never executed, although smaller teams from the Special Allied Airborne Reconnaissance Force (SAARF) were dropped near some camps to monitor the treatment of POWs from a distance.

Chapter Twenty-One

The Ruhr Pocket

Germany's industrial Ruhr region was manned by almost a third of a million German troops in early April 1945. They held in place as part of Hitler's no-retreat policy, which was particularly enforced in this critical manufacturing region. But the River Rhine had been breached by the Allies in several places. Tanks of the 2nd and 3rd armored divisions had met at Lippstadt, and the area behind them was now a pocket about half the size of New Jersey, containing the bulk of Field Marshall Model's Army Group B. Isolated in the pocket were the great industrial towns of Essen, Dortmund, and Dusseldorf, Germany. The 101st Airborne Div., minus the 501 was trucked up to hold the west bank of the Rhine River south of Dusseldorf in early April.

Raid on Himmelgeist

On several successive nights, each company of 1/506 sent patrols across the Rhine River. The patrols of B and C Companies were small in numbers of men involved, but the A Company crossing on the night of 11 April, was of company strength, supported by the 1/506 81mm mortar platoon, the 321st 75mm artillery, and some 155mm field artillery.

Don Straith, who joined the 506 before Bastogne and was wounded and evacuated at Noville, had rejoined the regiment. Part of his account of the company's raid follows:

After dinner on the 11th of April, we went back to our quarters, and with much laughing and horsing around, blackened our faces for the raid. In the

midst of this, someone bumped Santillan's mandolin from the windowsill, and it smashed on the pavement below. Although it could have been an omen of things to come, no one took it as such. We gathered our equipment and made our way to the company HQ at the edge of town.

We were briefed on our mission: cross the Rhine in small assault boats, proceed along a road and through a village [Himmelgeist], take what prisoners we could, and return in boats that the engineers would have waiting at the edge of the village. It now being dark, we hiked to the river road, turned upstream, and followed a curve to where our boats were waiting on the bank. As we assembled on the opposite shore a few minutes later, I became concerned about the amount of noise we were making and felt that a lot of men weren't taking this raid very seriously. When Syer said in a loud voice, "Where the hell is Straith?" I angrily hissed back, "Right behind you! Keep your damn voice down!"

When the last boats had landed a couple of minutes later, the company, with my squad as point, moved out on a road paralleling the river. The night was almost pitch-black, and men were bumping into each other with muttered oaths. This was soon followed by crashing sounds as we began tripping over and falling into small trees that the Germans had cut so as to land crosswise on the road. "So much for secrecy," I thought to myself. "If

Divisional HQ
Kangaroo sign outside HQ/101 in 1945. *Macri*

When we finally reached the edge of the village, we halted momentarily.

As we stood there, someone claimed to have detected a movement or light in the upstairs window of the first house, so we were ordered to put a rocket through it. Unfortunately, after loading the bazooka and trying several times unsuccessfully to fire it, we came to the conclusion that it was defective.

By this time, the other men in the company were moving around and through the village, so our squad and another one were told to set up a roadblock right where we were to protect our company's rear. From the road, a lane angled back toward a field, and we took up positions around where the two met. Syer, with that useless bazooka on his shoulder pointing down the lane, sat cross-legged behind a tree in the apex of the angle. The machine gun was set up on the right side of the tree, and Rex Runyan lay on the left with his rifle covering the way we had come. I lay behind Charlie, my head even with the feet of the men on either side. In a ditch to the rear, Santillan and Roberts waited with the BAR. The others took cover in and around the ditch where it passed under the lane. It's hard to say how long we waited there in the dark, the only sounds being distant shouts and an occasional shot from the rest of the company, as they swept through the town.

Suddenly, with only a fraction of a second warning, a salvo of shells bracketed our position, landing in the fields on either side and showering us with dirt. Ordered to hold our positions, we stayed where we were. The Germans must have really zeroed-in on us, because a couple of minutes later, there were explosions all around us as another salvo landed in our midst. I was frantically trying to stretch my steel helmet to cover all of me, when one shell burst a few feet to my left rear, and a chunk of compressed clay and stone from the roadbed hit my head. Through all the noise and shouting, I heard Syer call out, "Jerry, I'm hit bad!," and he fell over on his side and lay there groaning.

Elkins yelled, "Quick, Straith, put a tourniquet on my leg and get this damned machine gun off me." The concussion had blown his 42lb weapon, tripod and all, on top of him. To our surprise, Red and I were untouched, having been so close to where the shell landed that its fragments had arched just over us, one hitting Elkins and a bunch more tearing open Charlie Syer's back.

there are German troops here, they certainly know by now that we are coming."

The road turned north, and we had passed the last of the fallen trees, when from far out in a field to our left, a flare shot up and burst overhead. We froze—no time to hit the ground—and as we waited for the flair to burn itself out, I wondered if we were presenting a perfect silhouette to waiting enemy forces. Starting forward again, we had moved only a short distance when the order, "Halt!" rang out a few yards to our right. Instantly, almost every weapon in the point, except Syer's bazooka, fired in the direction of the voice. Before I could set down my two bags of rockets, the firing had ended and we could hear moaning out in the field. A couple of scouts moved out toward the sound, but the moans stopped. In the darkness, the unlucky sentry couldn't be found, so the column moved forward once more.

The shelling stopped and as I moved the machine gun, one of our medics ran up. After taking Syer's pulse and listening to him groan (Syer had also begun to gasp for air), the medic decided to take care of the other casualty instead.

Syer's groans were becoming weaker and then stopped altogether. I could see the luminous dial of his watch, so I reached for his wrist and felt his pulse, but after only a few beats it stopped also. When I reported this to the medic, he reached to check it himself and then confirmed that Charlie was dead. When the medic finished working on Elkins, we moved over to the ditch and found that the other medic, Alex Abercrombie, was also a casualty. Although up and about, he was bleeding from a temple wound, where a shell fragment had pierced the side of his helmet. After being bandaged, he was sent on ahead to where we were to meet the boats. A short time later, in view of our precarious position, the command was given for the rest of us to head through town to the boats, so we loaded Elkins on a stretcher, and started out.

As we moved along the road, I noticed the glow of a cigarette in the ditch and in a whisper asked the others who it was and why he was still there. Someone in the darkness replied that it was Roberts, that he was dying, and that the cigarette was all that could be done for him. His partner, Santillan I was told, had been hit in the middle of the back by one of the shells and blown in half. Leaving

Kickoff CP
Regimental CP of the 502 in the Ruhr Pocket. *White*

the two of them behind, we moved on toward the center of the village.

It was still pitch-black, and only a faint outline of the rooftops showed as a silhouette against the night sky. From the darkness ahead of us we heard a shout, crash, and much swearing as one of the men fell into a tank trap the Germans had dug

Platoon briefing in Germany, spring 1945. Members of 2nd Platoon of A/506, including Don Burgett. *Kennedy via Borelli*

Glidermen of B/327
A squad of glidermen from B/327 posed in the Dusseldorf area in April 1945. *Meeker*

across the road. If not for the noise he made, the four of us carrying the stretcher would have fallen in with our load. But we felt our way around the end of the hole, and a short way farther on, were directed down a lane on our left to the shore.

The boats were waiting as we were told, and we loaded the wounded man into one of them. Then we four knelt in the bottom of another, shoved off, and began paddling like mad. It was so dark that we couldn't see a thing, and we had no idea how far we had come or had to go when an explosion and a big orange fireball a few feet above the water lit up the river to our left. Whether it was from a tank or a field piece we didn't know, but the Germans had apparently rushed in some kind of artillery. This was presumably an 88, which was firing point-blank with shells timed to burst over our heads. Luckily, the current had carried our boat to one side of their line of fire, so we just crouched low and paddled faster. After half a dozen rounds, the firing stopped. Moments later, our boat ground to a sudden stop, and I had visions of us being stranded on a sandbar like sitting ducks. To our surprise and relief, we found we had safely reached the western shore again.

Dawn was breaking as we straggled back into Nievenheim. I was one of the first to reach our house and told Cofone about Syer, Santillan, and Roberts before going directly to bed. Later in the day we learned the results of the raid: three men dead, eleven others missing (including Abercrombie), and three prisoners. No one had seen Alex

after he had been sent on ahead to the boats. The other missing men were presumed to have drowned when their boats capsized.

The prisoners were all old men who could provide little if any information, and certainly weren't worth the men we had lost.

There wasn't much time to rest. That same day the company packed up again and moved about a mile north to the small village of Norf. Nothing eventful happened during our four days there except for the announcement of the death of President Roosevelt.

About a week after our ill-fated combat patrol, we got word that white surrender flags could be seen across the Rhine at Himmelgeist. When I heard that our company was to send a small party across to recover its three dead, I asked to go along, but was turned down. When the group returned later that day, they brought back four—not three—bodies from the common grave in which they had been buried by some Polish workers (all the German troops had pulled out of the area). Abercrombie, while on his way to the boats, had apparently passed out, bled to death, and was buried with the others. This closed the books on our Ruhr Pocket mission. Within a day or two we packed up once again and were taken by truck to a nearby railroad, where a long train of "40 & 8s" was waiting for us.

Landsberg Concentration Camp

As Allied forces swept into Germany in the final weeks of WWII, they began to liberate concentration camps and saw firsthand, brutal evidence of what the Nazis had done to enemies of the Reich. Most 101st troops were not directly involved in capturing any camps, although some troopers toured Dachau and other camps after they were freed by other units.

An exception was 1/506, as they discovered the camp at Landsberg. They had interrupted their dash toward Berchtesgaden in amphibious "Ducks" and disembarked after passing (and ignoring) long columns of surrendering German troops. Landsberg, Germany, was a town of approximately 25,000– 35,000 people, situated about 45 miles west of Munich. Hitler had been imprisoned there after his famous failed putsch and while there had written *Mein Kampf*.

Members of C/506 dismounted along the edge of a pine plantation, all the trees planted in neat rows with firebreaks between the sections and the trees all of a uniform height. A lengthy hike followed, ending at the concentration camp, which was situated just outside the town.

Kenneth Parker of C/506 described what transpired next:

We were told to deploy into the woods in a single column as deep as possible with approximately 20ft between us, then sweep forward, staying in contact with one another and searching for any personnel that could be hiding in the woods. My first shock occurred when I walked across the first opening. At the edge of the woods, there was a bush, perhaps 4ft high. Behind this bush was a skeleton in a crouching position. The skeleton wore the tattered striped purple garment of a Jewish concentration-camp member. I conjectured that he had either hidden here in order to escape, or in all modesty had gone behind the bush to go to the bathroom and had been too weak to return and died.

I went forward quite deep into the woods and could no longer see the road or the edge of the woods. As I progressed in my search, I began to feel very eerie; my senses were very acute in anticipation that something or someone would pop up in front of me at any minute. But something else was bothering me. As a young man (10–14 years old), growing up in upstate New York, I had a trap line that I tended each day. This necessitated daily trips through deep woods, and I was used to the sound of squirrels chattering, birds singing, ground animals scurrying away, wind blowing in the trees, and movement. I suddenly realized why I had the eerie feeling. There was no noise. There was no animal or bird life in the forest, and because of the needles on the forest floor, I could barely hear my own feet scuffling along, much less those of even the two troopers closest to me. I wondered if the Jewish concentration camp prisoners had worked in the forest and had killed and eaten every living animal and bird in order to stay alive.

After what seemed an hour or two of walking through the forest without incident, we came out on an open field with a slight mound across the road from what turned out to be a Jewish concentration camp. We swept the fields and headed for the open gates of the camp. Across from the gates, on this mound in the field, lay a dead German officer; from his epaulets I assumed he was an SS officer. He was stretched out on the ground face up, with the back of his head caved in. His boots and cap were missing when I went by. He was laying alongside a partially-dug grave. It looked as though he was having a Jew dig his own grave in front of the other prisoners across the street, when something distracted the German officer, and the Jew digging the grave hit

Rowing Across the Rhine
Members of A/506 went back to the Himmelgeist area to search for the bodies of men lost on the raid of 11 April. *Kennedy*

him in the back of the head with the shovel, grabbed the German hat and boots, and headed home.

In crossing Germany, we had seen many displaced persons (Poles, Czechs, etc.) that had one pair of boots or shoes on and another pair over their shoulder and they were walking home (hundreds of miles).

Most of the inmates had left, but passing the barracks we could see some of the weaker and sicker inmates still stretched out on their bunks. Our platoon was sent to a rather remote area of the camp to search for German soldiers. We followed a narrow-gauge railroad track, similar to the tracks miners use to push ore in a hopper to the outside. At the end of the track, there were approximately three holes, about 25ft long, maybe 20ft across. The holes appeared to have sloping sides that were cemented. Whether the bottoms of the holes were cemented, I don't know. Each of these holes, to whatever depth they were, were filled with bodies. None of the bodies had clothes on, and they all appeared to be in about the same state of deterioration. It was apparent that they were all Jews that had died. How many were in these three holes, I don't know. Later, I discovered that these were just surplus pits for the bodies until they could go into the huge furnaces that were farther down the track. I could see the smokestacks, but I never got into that area. The

Here Sleeps Four American Soldiers
The bodies of four A/506 men killed on the April patrol near Himmelgeist, Germany, were found and buried by the Germans. A patrol returned to the area to recover the bodies. The German inscription on the cross reads "Here sleep four American soldiers." *Kennedy*

huge furnaces were incapable of taking the bodies of all the dead Jews. They were loaded in the hoppers and dumped into the pits. This served as a waiting area, until the furnaces could take them, then the hoppers were reloaded with more bodies and pushed back down to the furnaces.

All of us, as we looked on the sight of all these bodies laying there in these three different pits, were quite shook up. We couldn't really fathom the enormity of it. Soon after seeing this, we were taken back outside the camp and went 6–8 miles to the town of Landsberg.

We were told that General Taylor, in view of what he had seen at the Jewish concentration camp, was pretty disturbed and had declared martial law in the entire area.

Robert Nelson and I were sent to Regimental HQ, where we received a detail to guard a crossroads.

Around 1030hr, we heard a huge noise; there were swarms of people coming out of the town in

Race to Berchtesgaden
Members of 2nd Platoon of A/506 aboard an amphibious "Duck" (DUKW) pause during the race to Berchtesgaden near Ludwigshofen, Germany. Justo Correa and Don Burgett are among those visible in the group. *Kennedy*

Landsberg Concentration Camp
The inhumanity of the Nazi regime was exemplified by the wretched victims found in concentration camps. This camp, east of Landsberg, was liberated by the 506. In addition to the emaciated starvation and typhus victims, the burned bodies were men who ran from a barracks set aflame by the SS and were mowed down by a machine gun. *US Army via Hood*

rows. It looked like 6,000–8,000 people heading toward the concentration camp, carrying rakes, brooms, shovels, whatever implements they could pick up. Some of the 101st guys were walking with them, keeping them in line and moving along. They said General Taylor had declared martial law, and issued an order that all people from age 14 to age 80 were to be rounded up out of Landsberg and marched through the concentration camp. They were to haul the bodies (what was left of them) out of the furnaces, haul the bodies out of all the holes, rake up the remains, and bury them all. Dig holes and bury them all.

That evening about 1800hr we saw the same crew of civilians coming back down the road from the concentration camp. Some of them were still puking; their hair was down. They were dirty. They did not look confident like they did when they went out. They looked totally distraught. I believe this process went on for several days while we were there.

General Taylor was so angry that he wanted these people never to forget what had been going on outside the town. Of course, they all pretended they didn't know what was going on. And I think probably they closed their eyes to a lot of it. The one thing I am sure of: the people in Landsberg, Germany, never forgot that experience.

A few days later we loaded back up on our "Ducks" and headed off down the road to Berchtesgaden. But nothing ever impressed in my mind a thought worse than what I had seen in Landsberg.

Chapter Twenty-Two

Berchtesgaden, Austria, and the End of the War

The Bavarian town of Berchtesgaden nestles amidst mountains and a landscape of breath-taking scenery in the southeast corner of Germany. Not far away are the Austrian and Swiss borders and the Brenner Pass to northern Italy.

Allied leaders still feared that Hitler might retreat to his Bavarian headquarters to command a last stand in the Alpine Redoubt. This fear proved unfounded, although many thousands of German troops had converged in the area, either in retreat from the Western Front or in flight from the Russians on the Eastern Front.

Hitler, Bormann, Goring, and others had luxurious homes in the Berchtesgaden area and below the Berghof, Hitler's mountain house, was a massive tunnel leading to subterranean chambers filled with liquor, silver services, fine crystal ware, and untold other loot. Hitler's library and numerous films and written records were also stored in his home away from Berlin.

Racing the French to Berchtesgaden

The entire area held a mystique and promise of discovery that drove the invading armies on in a relentless race to get there first. The 506 in their "Ducks" were at the vanguard of the 101st forces. Detouring around a blown bridge, flying down the autobahn past negligible resistance, they raced with the French 2nd Armored Div. to reach the prize.

The French columns were bypassed, only to overtake the American column a few hours later. Thousands of fully armed German soldiers were on the median of the autobahn, marching westward to surrender. The 506 met a delay when they had to obtain permission to pass through another division's sector. Then the race continued.

A platoon of C/506 reconned Berchtesgaden, but on the "Obersalzberg" slopes, the French had already arrived. Papers from the pillaged Berghof were already blowing across the mountainside. Such was the panorama when the first American troops arrived. Along with the 506th paratroopers came the 321st artillerymen and the 327th glider troops. Both the 501 and the 502 would arrive some weeks later.

But the complex was large enough that the French had only searched a part of it when the 506 joined the hunt with a vengeance. A huge wine cellar was discovered, and troops carried away armfuls of champagne and cognac. David Webster of E/506 later wrote that he was disappointed at the relatively cheap, recent-vintage liquors that were found there. Perhaps Hitler kept that supply only to entertain the nickel Nazis who visited there while hiding the better stuff elsewhere? In any case, Hitler himself was a teetotaler.

Another trooper remarked that it was "the ambition of every American paratrooper to drink Hitler's champagne." This being the case, troopers swarmed through the Berghof and its underground chambers in quest of the good stuff. In quest of booze, cupboards were pried open with silver table knives bearing Hitler's Eagle, swastika, and initials.

Some members of B/506 were exploring an underground tunnel below the Berghof when they encountered a locked room. Kicking open the door, the

American squad leaped inside, to find a Gruppen-fuhrer (major general of the SS) in full uniform standing in the room at attention. He was wearing a P-38 pistol in a holster at his hip.

The troopers drew down on him and demanded "Give us your pistol!"

"Nein!" shouted the SS general.

A paratrooper produced a cheap, small-caliber auto pistol and administered a shot to the general's ear. He went down, bleeding profusely and was dead within minutes. The troopers laid the general in a bed, removed all his insignia and decorations, then laid the cheap pistol in his hand. One of the troopers acquired the late general's P-38.

The squad moved on, and no one except those few who witnessed the incident actually knew what had happened. Dozens of troopers who arrived on the scene later have asked: "Did anyone ever mention the SS general who committed suicide below Hitler's house?" This myth has been further reinforced in a number of books and newspaper articles.

Another room down the hall was filled with silver cream pitchers, sugar bowls, serving trays, and the like, all emblazoned with Hitler's unique national emblem and the initials "A.H." Bob Reeves of B/506 brought an empty barracks bag into this room and filled it with silver items, then found it was too heavy to lift. He continued along, dragging the bag on the floor behind him. Later, while riding in a truck to Austria, Bob tossed pieces over each bridge as the truck crossed rivers and streams, to lighten the load. At this writing, he had given the last of the pieces away.

The Golden Age

The ensuing weeks became known as the "Golden Age" of the division, a reward for the hellish fighting of the previous year. Booze flowed, unofficial fraternization with the local girls was occasionally managed, luxury Nazi automobiles were liberated from their high-ranking owners, and horses were commandeered from the SS horse farm at Bruck, Austria, and galloped cowboy style.

In nearby fields, dozens of abandoned German armored vehicles and fighter planes were discovered, along with artillery, machine guns, and other assorted ordnance. There were the inevitable plane crashes, accidental shootings, and car crashes.

Some troopers had managed to take off in German planes but were killed while attempting to land them. A directive was issued banning attempts to fly these captured planes.

Himmler's Castle

Although the erstwhile home of Heinrich Himmler, the SS chief, was miles from Berchtesgaden at Zell am Zee, Austria, his castle at Bruck was the more intriguing feature of the area. This medieval, impressive Fischorn Castle, which was later

In the Eagle's Nest
The Adler Horst or Eagle's Nest, Hitler's hideout atop Kehlstein Mountain at Berchtesgaden. Note how small the men standing in the window look; this gives some perspective on the actual size of the building. *Nye*

used as Colonel Chase's CP, had served as a repository for Himmler's records and loot.

About a week before Allied troops arrived, Himmler's personal secretary Erika Lorenz had showed up at the castle with some trucks and a group of SS men. Acting under secret orders from Himmler himself, she had overseen the burning of numerous files and typewritten directives, some of which may have been written orders pertaining to the Final Solution policy toward Europe's Jewish population.

Fischorn Castle had also reportedly housed the valuables looted from concentration camp victims:

Hitler Hasn't Been Here Lately
Two new occupants relax in the Eagle's Nest. *Krochka*

Elevator to Hitler's Eagle's Nest
The elevator entrance to Hitler's Eagle's Nest was large enough to accommodate a vehicle. *Aprile*

Symbol of Tyranny
This intricately embroidered collar patch signifies the rank of Gruppenfuhrer (major general) in the SS. A member of B/506 cut this patch off the tunic of the general who was shot below the Berghof when he refused to surrender his pistol. The general was named Kastner, according to a newspaper item. *Author's collection*

large quantities of jewelry, paper money and coins of numerous countries and all denominations, gold teeth, and so on. This stolen treasure was allegedly divided into three parts. One third was discovered in a Bavarian cave within weeks by Seventh Army intelligence, who tracked it down through relentless interrogations and searches. They turned in an unknown percentage to be used in financing Cold War covert operations. Another third of the treasure is reportedly still secreted in the bottom of a lake nearby; numerous attempts to recover it in postwar years have produced negative results. Some divers have met mysterious "accidental" deaths while exploring the area.

The last third of the money and valuables was reportedly stashed in a location known only to a few high-ranking SS officers, including Col. Otto Skorzeny. He could access the money when it was needed to aid ex-Nazis, especially to pay legal expenses to defend accused war criminals.

Soon after the 506 arrived at Berchtesgaden, Sgt. Bill Knight of C/506 was told to accompany a major of Seventh Army Counter Intelligence Corps to the Fischorn Castle. Together they made one of the first searches of the castle. They forced their way into locked rooms and found, among other things, a trunk containing centuries-old looted paintings. In the rear of the castle were a number of newly built, garage-type structures in two rows, each one containing hoarded loot. One was filled with motorcycles. Another was full of small bins, containing all varieties of German political and military insignia, too much of it for a company of souvenir hunters to carry away. Knight grabbed a few hand-embroidered SS officer sleeve eagles as a curiosity and left the rest.

Much like the loot in the Berghof, all the loot in the various garages would eventually disappear in thousands of different directions.

The Day the War Ended

On the afternoon of 8 May, the day the war officially ended in Europe, Bill Knight was sent on another mission with two jeeploads of personnel from the 506.

They had received word that an entire Wehrmacht division plus stragglers from assorted units was waiting in fields near Bad Gastein for instructions to demobilize and surrender. The 506ers located the German division and conferred with its commanders, who were living in a large mobile house trailer. The paratroopers spent the night in the trailer, and in the morning had the German commander instruct his troops to "disarm, go to Salzberg, and then go home." Knight and his buddies stood at the edge of the road as thousands of fully armed German soldiers walked up out of the field, dropped their weapons in a ditch at the side of the road, then turned down the road, walking toward Austria.

Still Smokin'
The Berghof, Hitler's luxurious mountain house, was still smoking from bombing raids when the 101st arrived. A massive underground tunnel complex lay beneath the house and yielded many secrets and treasures to the conquering troops. *Musura*

There would be no out-processing nor imprisonment for these troops.

An SS officer walked up to Sergeant Knight, handed him a ceremonial dagger with a chain hanger depicting skulls and lightning bolts and said, "A souvenir . . ."

He then turned and joined the horde of marching, defeated troops.

Back at Berchtesgaden

Back at the Berghof complex at Berchtesgaden, an SS guard barracks that stood near Hitler's house had been placed off limits. The windows were boarded-up, the electricity inside was turned off, and the floor was flooded with a foot of water. A few enterprising troopers from the 501 pried a board loose and went inside to explore. They had no flashlight and resorted to striking matches in the darkness. They found lockers full of uniforms, photos and papers, also numerous insignia. The rifle racks were still full of Mauser rifles. The troopers took as much as they could carry but later lamented that they didn't have more illumination to aid in their search. The contents of that building also evaporated in the coming weeks.

Hitler's house and some of the adjoining buildings had been damaged by Allied bombers before

Jim Cox
Lieutenant Jim Cox of C/326 in Normandy, 1944. Cox, formerly a first sergeant, was commissioned on the battlefield. *Crilley*

Hitler's Car
Hitler's Mercedes was liberated at Berchtesgaden by Lt. Jim Cox of C/326; he also had the honor of touring the states with the vehicle to sell War Bonds. *Cox*

the 101st arrived, but some distance away was a complex of modern Alpine barracks also used by SS troops. These became the new home of the 501 when they rejoined the division following the scrubbing of Operation Jubilant.

Up at the top of neighboring Kehlstein Mountain was Hitler's conference building, known as the Adlerhorst (Eagles Nest), but referred to by many troopers as the "Crow's Nest." This impressive building stood at the peak of the mountain and was partly accessible by a large elevator that could carry vehicles most of the way up the mountain. Ted Goldman of A/502 recalled some details of the period that followed the surrender of the 13th SS Panzer Korps (excerpted from the *Chappie Hall Newsletter* #12, 28 August 1969):

In May 1945 A/502 was stationed at Reit im Winkel, Bavaria, with the rest of 1/502. For three weeks following VE-day, one of our chores was standing guard with and on 5,000 German remnants of the SS. Outposts were usually in the country or on the edge of a village. The Germans had bolt-action rifles and wore white armbands. They were supposed to control German traffic. We were on nearby outposts, usually 100yd away. Our job was to keep the German outposts honest.

During May, the Bavarian nights are cold. For a week or so the Germans moved to the American outpost after dark. We sent them to the sawmill regularly for firewood and practiced our "tradin Ger-

Soaking Up the Sun
Soaking up some Bavarian sunshine in one of the lounge chairs used by Hitler's staff and visitors at the Eagle's Nest is Pat Macri, Division Signal Company. Macri is enjoying the feeling of victory after a hard war. *Macri*

An old German Jager, or hunter, led Joe Pistone (left) and Lindfield to an SS hideout in the mountains where more die-hards were captured. *Pistone*

man" after dark. One evening, Lieutenant Colonel Hanlon had a battalion meeting in which he was rather definite about there being no further fraternization, particularly at the sawmill. At 0600 the next morning, Charles "Greek" Sakalakos and I arrived at the sawmill outpost for our 4hr turn. A short while later . . . the longest touring car still operating in Europe drove up. I stopped it. It contained three Germans: the driver, a master sergeant and two officers. The officers were a colonel who spoke excellent and polite English and an exceedingly fat lieutenant general, complete with lap robe, baton, and red lapels.

In response to my request for passes, the driver and the colonel produced valid I.D. documents properly signed by Col. Ned Moore, 101st Chief of Staff. The general refused to answer and did not turn or indicate in any way that he heard me. A second request brought only the colonel's response that his pass was good for the general, too. We were already in trouble with Long John for fraternization, so I wasn't about to let anyone by without seeing his pass.

GIs have a dislike for generals, which comes naturally, and in May 1945, two GIs had their con-

centrated on the general at hand. I was standing in the middle of the road, and the Greek was on the other side, near the general. I told the general to produce a pass or dismount. He did neither. I told

Medieval Masterpiece
Shown here is one of the scores of rare paintings stolen by Hermann Goering from various European museums. Troopers of the 101st discovered the cache of artwork hidden in the Berchtesgaden area and put the paintings on display for visiting troops while trying to inventory the works and return them to their former owners. *Meeker*

Tanker of the French 2nd Armored Div., talking with a member of HQ/101 in Berchtesgaden. *Macri*

Home of the 506
Signs like this proliferated in Austria after VE-Day. *Moulliet*

Sakalakos to fix his bayonet and nudge the general into obedience. By the time he had his bayonet in place, the door between the general and Sakalakos was open. The smallest nip showed the general that we meant business. The general dismounted, the colonel turned purple, the sergeant about choked, either with suspense or mirth, I wasn't sure.

The general produced his pass, at the same time stating in perfect English that he had never been so insulted and that General Taylor would immediately hear about this. I pointed out politely that a prompt and polite response to a legal request would have saved him a lot of trouble. The general turned to remount. The sight of that massive bottom

was too much for the Greek. Although short, Greek was strong and quick. He used the flat of his boot to the greatest advantage and landed a resounding smack across the backside of that mound of Nazi blubber. The general came hurtling across the width of the back seat, where he hit the inside of the door face first and collapsed in a heap on the floor. Since I was standing facing that door, I shall never forget the look of shocked amazement on the flying walrus' face. The colonel turned even darker purple, leaped into the car to pick up the general, and yelled at the driver to go, all in one motion. I collapsed in the middle of the road in gales of laughter, completely out of action. Whatever happened now would be anticlimactic. All Sakalakos could say was, "Fat German bastard."

Within 20min, the phone started ringing. The officer at the CP asked, "What the hell have you guys been up to?"

I replied, "Nothing, why?"

"The Captain is on his way after having had calls from Division, Regiment, and Battalion."

In 5min, Captain Swanson and his driver showed up. Swanie reamed us out good, but without his usual gusto. He was even smiling when he left. No one ever mentioned the general. Makes you wonder . . .

General Tolsdorf The Mad
Tolsdorf, a reknowned German Panzer commander (second from right), surrenders his troops to Col. Bob Sink of the 506 (center). *Mihok*

Although the non-fraternization policy was difficult to enforce, some troopers were officially punished for having German girlfriends, but this did not deter some troopers. Sergeant Jimmy Edgar of I/501 had returned from his Alsace wounding as he had vowed to do and now had two "shack rats" in the Berchtesgaden area: Ischi and Uscha, who had been Heinrich Himmler's teletype operators.

Patrols went into the neighboring mountains, and several Nazi war criminals were rounded up, including Karl von Oberg, former Gestapo chief of Paris, Labor Minister Robert Ley, and the infamous Jew-baiter Julius Streicher.

It seemed fitting that the weary survivors of the 101st spent the end of the war lounging in Hitler's furniture and grabbing their share of the plunder that was abundant in the Berchtesgaden area.

On 26 June 1945 the 501 was inactivated, and the high-point men were sent back to the States. The others were shipped to the 327, the 502, and the 506 and integrated into companies in those units. To help add points toward discharge, a Bronze Star was awarded to all men who had made the three major missions of the 101st: Normandy, Holland, and Bastogne.

Surrendering Elite Guard
These two Waffen SS enlisted men belonged to the 13th SS Panzer Korp. Here, in May 1945 at Kossin, Austria, they surrender to the 502. The man at right wears a black Panzer wrap-around tunic with shoulder straps from the officer cadet school at Bad Tolz. *White*

Spoils of War
A massive pile of helmets, rifles, and sundry equipment from the surrendering 13th SS Panzer Korp in Kosin, Austria. One wonders what happened to it all. *White*

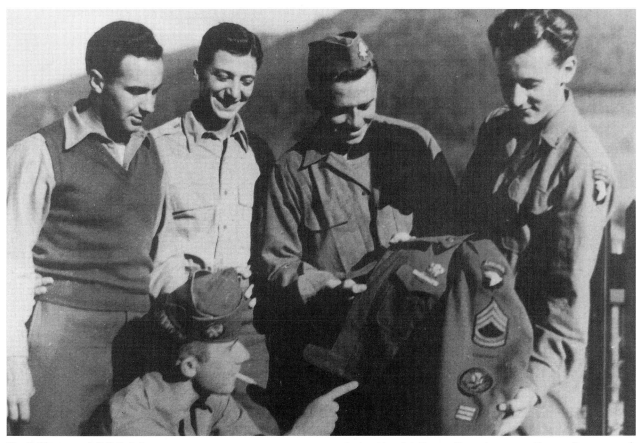

Cecil Simmons' S-2 Patch
The green sleeve patch designed by Lt. Col. Cecil Simmons for wear by his S-2 personnel is shown here. Dick Ladd (cap on sideways) points to the patch, which was laid on the sleeve of Gordon "Bill" Little's Ike jacket for the photo. He didn't sew it on because it wasn't approved. There is only one known instance of the patch being sewn onto a wartime uniform. Also pictured from left to right are Jack Ott, Bill Farrington, and Roger Flurscheim. *Ladd*

Assignments followed, sending the 101st to Auxerre, France, where a pay jump was made in September, and to Sens and Joigny, France. Many troopers visited Paris and the Riviera. It was a peri-od of marking time before the happy return to the States and discharge from the Army.

Bill Russo In Paris

Lieutenant Bill Russo got into Paris after VE-day, with a replacement officer named Koenig. Russo recalled:

> Koenig and I were sitting in one of those side-walk cafes, and about 100yd away is the Arc de Triomphe. Well, we didn't have too much faith in the French Army. The way they line up for battle, they have a jeep, two trucks full of chickens, broads, one tank destroyer . . . you think I'm joking, don't you, huh? Well I've got news for you. There's no joke. This is their attack plan, OK?

> Well, Koenig and I were discussing various things and someone must have mentioned those French, you know, because they were never there. Never. We were pretty juiced-up. Koenig gets up, walks over to the Arc de Triomphe, and pisses on it.

An assembly center at Namur, Belgium, had a large movie screen set up to entertain troops awaiting shipment back to the States. The photo was made by Charlie Placidi of the 907. *Placidi*

At one of the track and field events soon after VE-Day, Gen. George Patton and Gen. Maxwell Taylor are visible in the center of the photo. At bottom center is Maj. Richard J. Allen (wearing sunglasses) and Capt. Hugo S. Sims, both of whom served with the 501 in combat. *via Meeker*

Broad daylight! There was a riot! I never saw Koenig again. Boy he was tough, God he was a tough man. He was one of the few people I would really be hesitant about meeting. That guy was something else.

Homecoming

Although the Screaming Eagles—who had covered themselves in glory in Normandy, Holland, and Bastogne—had looked forward to a triumphant homecoming and a victory parade down New York's Fifth Avenue or perhaps Washington's Pennsylvania Avenue, this was not to be. The 101st was inactivated on 30 November 1945 in Auxerre, France. The veterans who had served the 101st Airborne so well in combat returned to the States piecemeal, in various other units. A relative handful came back with the 82nd Airborne and got the honor of marching down Fifth Avenue in their victory parade.

The 101st would remain dormant until the early 1950s when it was used as a basic training unit at Camp Breckenridge, Kentucky, during the Korean War. The division was not reactivated in all its glory as a full-fledged airborne division until 1956. It has

served at Ft. Campbell, Kentucky, ever since, with considerable combat time in the Vietnam and Gulf wars.

Lieutenant Corey Shepard of I/502 wrote a few thoughts about postwar readjustment:

Pulling into New York Harbor after passing the Statue of Liberty was an unforgettable sight for millions of returning Americans in September 1945. *Probst*

157

Relaxation Time
Members of the 506's S-2 and S-3 sections relax in Austria in the summer warmth of 1945. *Chwastiak*

In memory of Helen Briggs-Ramsey, known as Briggsy, Red Cross girl for the 506. Helen was tragically beaten to death in her Capitol Hill, Washington, D.C. apartment days before the 50th Anniversary of D-Day in June 1994. She was loved by many and will be mourned by all who knew her. *Yates*

The veteran returns from battle, and wondrous sights of courage that no knight of old, no cowboy, no serial hero ever dreamed of. Fighting wounds that heal slowly, school, interest rates, the thousand trials of feeding those mouths everyday—all require a different skill and a painstaking patience harder than patrol in enemy country because it's dull and you can't kill your enemies, only cope with them. These were men. Where others feared to go, they leapt. When others saw them, secret envyings ate at them. If there be nobility in such things as strength and bravery and self sacrifice, then these are princes of rare blood. If legends are made of this stuff, then these— for whom Alexander's, Caesar's, and Napoleon's legions could not be link-boys—these Battered Bastards can't fade away.

Index